The Beverly Hills Style

Also by Judy Mazel

THE BEVERLY HILLS DIET
THE BEVERLY HILLS DIET LIFETIME PLAN

The Beverly Hills Style

HOW TO BE
THE STAR
IN YOUR OWN LIFE

JUDY MAZEL

STEIN AND DAY/*Publishers*/New York

First published in 1985
Copyright © 1985 by Judy Mazel
All rights reserved, Stein and Day, Incorporated
Designed by Louis A. Ditizio
Printed in the United States of America
STEIN AND DAY/*Publishers*
Scarborough House
Briarcliff Manor, N.Y. 10510

Library of Congress Cataloging in Publication Data

Mazel, Judy.
    The Beverly Hills style.

    1. Success.   2. Mazel, Judy.   I. Title.
BJ1611.2.M36   1985   646.7   84-40626
ISBN 0-8128-3001-6

Because of you . . .

Margie and Herman Platt
Cindy Griffith Wayne
Arnie Rothlisberger
Mike Cohn
James Jennings Sheeran
Esther Mazel

And I never could have done it without your help . . .

Bootsie Barth, Jim Flaherty, Sam, Liz Kelly, Patricia Day, Ellen Hexom, Allen Allen, Loren Davis, Mindy Weiss, Ed Radisch, Lydia Bach, Elizabeth Halfpapp and their Tuck Release Team, Nell Yperifanos, Dario Mariotti, Paul Madson and their set, cast, and crew, Leslie Rodger, Olga Mendell, Martin Shrader, John Bacco, Carl Maione, John Goonan, Bennie Jordan, Bobby Egan, James Kenny, George Davis, the boys at Kaplans, the kids at KHS, Jerry Bishop, Fred DeBellis and my little baby brother, Richard Dombroff, Anne Bates, Joseph Benti, Diana Okula, Gus Ober, Debra Gonzalez, and the Fleet at Flynns

This is not a book on social etiquette but a guide for people who live, as we all do, in the ruthlessly competitive, upwardly mobile world of today. I've written it to show you how to win as I have won, how to come out ahead in every social and personal situation you encounter. How to be the STAR in your own life.

Judy Mazel

Contents

Introduction:
A Star Is a Wish to
Build a World Upon

Welcome to the world of dreams come true—to the land of milk and honey. Welcome to the world of getting what you want. A world where no star is too far away, where there is no fantasy that can't become reality. Ask and ye shall receive! Welcome to a way of living I call the Beverly Hills Style.

She walks into a room and she owns it. It really doesn't matter that she's forty pounds overweight and her daily coiffed hair looks as if she's slept in it; there's a hush as she walks through the door. He gets fired; it's been on television, made the headlines—it's humiliating. No, it's not—not for him. He goes to Friday lunch at Ma Maison, the chicest place to be, and, as he enters, the crowd stands up to cheer him. They're the Beverly Hills Winners!

How do they do it? How do they get away with it? They've *learned* how, that's how. They've learned a secret that you're about to learn. They have discovered that certain special something that sets some people glowingly apart from others. You've seen it over and over again—that certain special difference, that elusive quality that's hard to define if you don't have it because it's a tantalizing mixture of so many things. It's flair and it's presence. It's radiance and it's charisma. It's a magic state of being that's been perfected on the world's largest, most prestigious stage, Beverly Hills.

It's technique!

Beverly Hills, where the sun shines every day, and age is ageless. Where it's today that counts, not yesterday. Where no one really cares from whence you came but only that you're there. Where roots and family tree have no bearing on the fruit, for we are all saplings—first-generation superstars in the sunshine of today. Riding the high of our hit song, our megabuck movie deal, our top-rated TV show. From nobodies to the most wanted. You don't really think anyone was *born* in those iron-gated houses north of Sunset, do you?

As you timidly peer through the doorway of the Polo Lounge, you are aware that only one mood prevails. The room is abuzz—the tables are filled with stylish little groups flaunting their flair and savoir-faire.

Look over there! Last night she was toting spareribs at Tony Roma's, chewing gum, and wisecracking with her customers. Tonight, well, you'd think she was the star of a hit television series. And over there! A bottle of Cristal champagne is on his table, his shirt open at the neck, glistening with all the gold chains; six zeros follow every figure you overhear. A top producer celebrating his success? You're wrong. He hasn't made the year's biggest-grossing film—he's actually an agent-in-training, a mail boy at the William Morris Agency.

What makes them so believable, these shining people? They have a style! A style that turns dreams into reality. A style that is going to move them right into an iron-gated house. They've seen it happen. They remember when Diana Ross came from the Detroit ghetto. They watched her take the trip . . . of success. Sure the stars come and go, but most of them came from somewhere else—Nowhere, Idaho. They came into the world naked, and now they're sporting minks and diamonds. They've made it happen. They've made themselves into what they are. They've watched, they've studied, they've adopted, and they've adapted. They've grown up in the aura of the silver screen. They've created their own characters and now they are writing their own scripts. Just as you will begin to do once I've taught you how. In the beginning, I'll be writing the scripts for you, but by the time you've finished this book and rehearsed and played out the scenes, you'll be doing it all on your own. Because if they can do it, and if I can do it, so can you.

You see, I'm not really any different than you. I'm just a formerly fat girl from Chicago who had a dream. Well, perhaps there is one difference—I've made my dream come true. When I was young I would sit alone for hours fantasizing about famous people. Someday! Someday! I wanted to be rich and famous, successful, and powerful. And I wanted to be loved. Well, I got everything I wanted. How did I do it? Trust me, there is no magic, it's technique. I observed, I studied, I adopted, and I adapted.

The stars on the silver screen were my first teachers—I spent hours as a child at the movies, studying. Later it was my Beverly Hills clinic, where I treated many of my early idols as well as the most famous of today's world. Still later, I had a bird's-eye view: for two years I lived in the hub of it all, the Beverly Hills Hotel. But that was just my training period.

I didn't perfect my technique in one fell swoop, nor will you. It was trial and error, experience and experiment. It took years. It'll be easier for you, though, because there will be my script for every situation—from improving your image to getting whatever you want in a restaurant. Heaven knows, you'll make a few mistakes along the way, but that's what's going to make it fun. That's how you'll learn. Listen, if you knew all the answers, if you knew how to get IT, then you wouldn't need this book.

Believe me, I've made my share of mistakes along the way. I'll never forget being at a very elegant dinner party with one of the richest, most eligible bachelors in London. He had very honorable intentions and was introducing me to his closest friends. On my right was the head of Lloyds of London; on my left, the Chancellor of the Exchequer. As I served myself the brussels sprouts, they went in every direction except my plate—the lap of the gentleman on my left, the lap of the gentleman on my right. Some even rolled across the table, to the shocked horror of my intended. . .

Disaster, you think? The end of everything? Wrong. Romance didn't end, nor did I fall out of favor with the other dinner guests. *Au contraire;* I simply laughed and asked for more. I had the dignity and aplomb to pull it off with style. A style I first developed in Beverly Hills, then later perfected in the European playgrounds.

Little fat Judy no more, I had become an expert. I had been moving with the movers and shakers—and matching them move for move, and shake for shake.

Just a few short years ago I had barely seen the United States, no more than a handful of cities. Today I've crisscrossed America five times and been around the world—several times—staying in only the grandest hotels. For the past year my home base has been the grandest of them all, Claridge's in London. The meeting place of the crème de la crème—royalty, heads of state, and the international set. This has been my postgraduate course, the ideal finishing school.

Without planning to, I've taken an advanced course in Style. You see, my best-selling book opened every door to me, the most important in the world. From the exclusive shops on Rodeo Drive to the Paris salons of old-line aristocrats to Roman palazzi . . . I've been the house guest of a duke and duchess in their Scottish castle, the closest confidante of an aging German princess, the lover of lords, barons, and European superstars.

I lived through a social whirl of diplomatic dinners, hunts, shoots, skiing holidays, and yacht cruises. And, during them all, I looked, I listened—and I learned. And now I'm going to teach you *what* I learned as I observed those privileged men and women and how they get away with it.

I've seen that what comes naturally to those born into it is really nothing more than a highly polished version of the Beverly Hills Style. What you'll learn is a synthesis of both worlds, the world of natural style and the world of applied style. Because that's exactly what the Beverly Hills Style is—applied style—and it's an art that can be learned, an art you will easily master. It will allow you to turn defeat into victory, to propel yourself to top management, marry the President of the United States, sleep with film stars—or to not do anything you don't want to do.

It won't matter that you don't live in Beverly Hills, or that you don't go to formal dinner parties. Well, haven't you ever had embarrassing moments at Kentucky Fried Chicken? Haven't you ever regretted not saying what you "should have" to a gas station attendant? Haven't you ever resented someone else's getting a table in a restaurant before you? Style is not the exclusive property of princesses or countesses. In fact, it doesn't depend at all on birth, wealth, or good looks; where you live or what you do for a living. Of course any of these can give you a better starting position, but they really are irrelevant. Whoever you are, whatever you do, wherever you live, you are about to win your rightful place in life—and life in the sunshine of popularity and success. Get your own way and get away with it. I'm going to show you how.

Believe me, nothing is impossible. Nine years ago I was skateboarding on the boardwalk in Venice, California, wondering what to do with my last 75 cents. Should I buy food, toilet paper, or a beer? Today—well, today the big question is do I buy that $13,000 Valentino dress?

My success came from believing it could happen. Over and over I'm asked, "Are you surprised at the success of your book?" With all due modesty, though I am, I must admit that I must have known it would happen. A bridge isn't built before it's someone's idea. A skyscraper can't be erected before someone designs it. And your life can't take shape or form until you have the mold. Create a dream, and it can become your reality. Create your life, and it will become it. Know what you want and you will get it.

But perhaps you're not sure what it is you want. You've dared not let yourself think or dream about it. *It*, the illusive *It*. Love, Money, Power, Fame, Success, and everything that goes along with them. It's what we're all after! And now it can all be yours. I'm going to give you the tools and guide your hand as you pour in the foundation. And then, brick by brick—or should I say script by script, as you'll see in the next chapter—you'll build a whole new world. A world in which you can have anything you want because the plan that's going to make it possible, the mortar that's going to hold it all together, is the Beverly Hills Style.

William Shakespeare said, all the world's a stage, and we are merely players. So let's have fun and let's make it a grand performance.

THIS IS YOUR LIFE, SO START LIVING!

Scripts for Living

Nothing is achieved without effort. Just *reading* this book will not give you Beverly Hills Style; you will also have to *practice* it. I'm going to tell you how it's done, but perfecting The Beverly Hills Style is going to require concentrated hard work. Think of your favorite film stars; do you think they just move from part to part? They study, they rehearse, and they live the part before they become that person you believe them to be on the screen.

I know you probably never thought of yourself as an actor/actress, and you've probably never even considered going to acting school. Well, that's basically what you're going to do, only it's a home study course. You see, developing The Beverly Hills Style is acting, acting the star role of yourself.

Within each chapter you will find scenes, scenes that set up situations that put you in a time and place. I'll give you a script and a dialogue to rehearse. I'll even give you the objective that you and the scene are intended to accomplish. Then it will be up to you to act them out for real. Most of the situations will happen naturally; the other characters will cast themselves. Some situations, however, you will have to create. Some of the characters you will have to cast. But the star will almost always be you.

The scenes and the scripts are not unlike acting exercises. You have enrolled in an acting class (well, you're reading this book, aren't you?), but it's not one that is confined within four walls, directed by a coach, and shared with other students. Here you are the lone star student, and your rehearsal stage is the world.

It's hardest at first. In the beginning you'll feel as if you're acting. But as any coach will tell you, when you are truly playing a scene you're not aware of yourself in that scene. If you are aware of yourself you're not doing it, you're judging. While you're doing it, you should be wholly concentrated on what you're doing. The time to judge comes later, when you've seen the reactions you've obtained and the effect you've had on others. *Then* you can judge your performance and score yourself. This won't happen overnight. In the beginning you'll probably be conscious of your every blink, every word. As you begin to relax, as you trust, and as you believe, it will all begin to happen naturally.

The chapters and scenes are all in progressive order, so it is important that you not skip anything or do anything out of context. As in a play or a film, each scene relates to the next. They will only all work together in the order in which they are presented.

The scenes, by the way, are all worthy of an award-winning performance; I've named each of them after a film or a song that has won an Oscar.

Trust me, trust the scenes, and trust yourself. Soon there will be nothing conscious, nothing "acted" about the way you behave. It will become what you are, your style. And The Beverly Hills Style will become you.

2

A Star Is Born

ACT I   **PROPS:** Pencil
                                        Small notebook
                                        Mirror

There is no one like you. You are special—you are unique. The Beverly Hills Style is not a thing, it's a way of being. To acquire it, you must first take a long hard look at yourself; identify who and what you are, accept what makes you unique, and cultivate it.

The Beverly Hills Style is a lifegame that anyone can win, that *you* can win, as long as you believe that you're good enough. The only thing that can hold you back is you. All that you are is what you think you are. What you think of yourself is what others think of you. If you have always considered yourself boring, or dumb, or ugly, then you have been just that. Well, if that's what you thought, how could you have been anything else?

Regardless of what you have thought of yourself in the past, it is in the past. You are about to develop a whole new image, a whole new sense of self. When you begin to recognize yourself as the superior person you are, you will become that superior person. You see, there is nothing about you that need be negative: every characteristic has its good and bad side. Any negative, any of your flaws, can be turned into a positive, into an attribute. When you begin recognizing a negative as a quality rather than a flaw, that's what it will become. Let me show you what I mean:

THE BEVERLY HILLS STYLE

NEGATIVE	POSITIVE
Boring	Misunderstood
Dull	Solid
Crass, crude	Forceful
Vulgar	Extroverted
Loud	Uninhibited
Argumentative	Questioning
Stupid	Unaffected
Clumsy	Dreamy
Vain	Self-assured
Unimaginative	Sensible
Uptight	Reserved
Nervous	High-strung
Shy	Mysterious
Overexcitable	Extroverted
Quiet	Thoughtful
Gushy	Affectionate
Shallow	Light
Intolerant	Truthful
Short-tempered	Emotional
Rude	Forthright
Superficial	Light
Deceitful	Self-preserving
Boastful	Self-assured
Easily hurt	Sensitive
Neurotic	Changeable
Hysterical	High-strung
Mean	Direct
Unkind	Honest
Egocentric	Self-aware
Weak	Guileless
Ineffectual	Placid
Wasteful	Extravagant
Self-centered	Self-aware
Uninteresting	Misunderstood
Sloppy	Casual
Careless	Carefree

NEGATIVE	POSITIVE
Obnoxious	This is too general a description. Please decide just what it is about you that is obnoxious
Thoughtless	Carefree
Forgetful	Dreamy
Inhibited	Reserved
Mousy	Natural
Gluttonous	Pleasure-seeking
Overbearing	Forceful
Pushy	Determined
Selfish	Self-preserving
Silly	Guileless
Moody	Sensitive
Willful	Determined
Immature	Innocent
Talkative	Gregarious
Inconsiderate	Self-preserving

Scene 1. **JOURNEY INTO SELF**
Objective: To Confront, Acknowledge, and Let Go

In the space below or in a separate workbook (one you've made yourself or The Beverly Hills Stylebuilder workbook—see p. 263), I want you to list all the things you hate about yourself.

"THINGS I HATE ABOUT MYSELF" LIST

Scene 2. **ACCENTUATE THE POSITIVE**
Objective: To Turn a Negative Quality into a Positive Quality
with the Help of Semantics

In the space below, or in your workbook, I want you to write, in
sentence form, the positive equivalent of all your negatives. Precede
the negative with "I'm not..." and the positive with "I am..." For
example: "I'm not quiet, I'm mysterious. I'm not inhibited, I'm
reserved." If you have trouble finding a positive equivalent for
anything, check my list; I made it particularly long to cover all
bases. If you are something I missed, I'm sure you'll find a reasonable facsimile.

"I'M NOT... I AM..." LIST

List in hand, go stand in front of the mirror. Look yourself
straight in the eye and declare what you aren't and what you are.
Just read the list aloud.

Scene 3. AN AFFAIR TO REMEMBER
Objective: To Fall in Love with Yourself

There are many reasons for people to admire you, but how can they be expected to do so until you recognize and admire yourself? Okay, clear your mind. Consider yourself calmly and dispassionately. Then underline the words below that best describe you. Now that you have begun to realize what a terrific person you are, I'm sure you'll find a few.

"ALL THE THINGS I AM" LIST

enthusiastic	sympathetic	poised	intelligent	energetic
quick-thinking	hard-working	creative	instructive	loyal
imaginative	logical	thoughtful	studious	assertive
friendly	witty	relaxed	generous	confident
quiet				

All right, it's back to the mirror again. That's right, look yourself straight in the eye and *really* let yourself know how terrific you are. Repeat all the words you've underlined, preceding them with "I am."

Scene 4. DECISION BEFORE DAWN
Objective: To End and Begin Each Day on a Positive Note about You

Wait a minute, we're not through yet. You still might not be convinced. There's one more step, and that's letting the positive put you to sleep at night. Take your workbook and write down all the "I am's" from your "I'm not ... I am ..." list. Add all the traits you have just underlined from your "All the Things I Am" list, adding "I am" before them. Take your workbook to bed with you each night, and, right before you close those little eyes, recite the list aloud. And just so you start each day on a positive note, you'll do the same thing when you wake up. Your workbook should be small enough to fit in your purse or your pocket and should be carried with you at all times. You just never know when you might need a reminder!

Before you know it, these positive qualities won't be strangers. They are you, and they become you. Study them. Consider them. They are of great value. They are your *most* precious assets. As you begin to employ them, to use them, like muscles they will improve and grow stronger with deliberate use. As with a talent, as in a sport, deliberate conscious daily practice will improve their function—your function.

ACT II   **PROPS: Pencil**
                          Notebook

Scene 1. **THE FACTS OF LIFE**
Objective: The Confirmation of Your Positive Qualities by Your Intimates

There's nothing better than someone else telling you how wonderful you are. Now that you know what you think of yourself—now that you know all the fine things you are—it's time for someone else to tell you, too. For most of us, it's not only our self-perception that holds us back, it's our misconception of what we think other people think of us—that we don't live up to their expectations. Well, I think you just might be in for a few surprises.

Ask the five most important people in your life the three things they like best about you. Come on, it's not as hard as it sounds! Remember, these are people who are important to you, you must mean something to them. There must be some things about you that they like!

It's best to do this in person, face to face, but if you are too embarrassed, the telephone will do. No letters, please, unless all other forms of communication are impossible. I want you to revel in the glory, glow in the sunshine of their words, and get off on yourself.

SCRIPT: You need no preliminaries, no explanations. In the course of conversation you will simply say, "I've been wondering, what are the three things you like best about me?"

When they've told you, it's not necessary to comment or to compliment them back. Just listen—I mean really listen—then simply say "Thank you" and delight in the positive feedback. Know that this is just the beginning of what is going to be a steady stream of compliments. When you get home, fill in a Positive Feedback Prompter in your workbook (see example below).

You have one week to act out this scene. If you don't see your Big Five frequently, then either arrange a meeting or make a phone call. You cannot go any further until this is completed—so hurry up.

Well, haven't you wasted enough years of your life already?

POSITIVE FEEDBACK PROMPTER

NAME:
RELATIONSHIP:
3 THINGS HE/SHE LIKES BEST ABOUT ME:

    1. _____
    2. _____
    3. _____

I THOUGHT SO   ☐
I WAS SURPRISED   ☐
I WAS DISAPPOINTED*   ☐

***Well, what did you expect?**

If you come up with anything new, anything you didn't already know, add it to your "I am" List. You can add to that list any time you discover something new and wonderful about yourself. That's what it's for. Use it to reinforce your ego and self-esteem whenever you feel insecure.

ACT III   **PROPS:** Pencil
                             Notebook
                             Telephone directory
                             Telephone
                             Money

Scene 1. **BORN FREE**
Objective: To Eliminate the Idea That Your Past Has Any Bearing
        on Your Future

Though they will deny it, most people are social snobs. Though you may protest the opposite, you're just as bad. You believe there is a magic world that belongs to the rich and powerful and well-born. Well, you're right, it does belong to the rich and powerful, but birthright has absolutely nothing to do with it. And, I might add, though you need not have the same background to mix with them, you just must be as confident of your background as they are of theirs.

Americans live in a fluid and mobile society in which there is no social background that is "better" than any other. There is no place, no class, no geographical area that cannot be made into an advantage. There is no origin that when used positively cannot be a positive-plus. There is no need ever to be embarrassed by your background. Don't try to hide your roots—major in them. Exaggerate them. Always remember, they are you—the wonderful person you are. Don't try to hide your origin, don't minimize it. The more humble your beginnings, the greater you are today. Remember, we are all saplings, first-generation superstars.

- The first Astor was a German butcher.
- The Rothschilds originated in a ghetto and took their name from the street they lived on.
- The Gabor family, all of whom are now celebrities, came from a modest background in Budapest.
- Perhaps you have something in common with Walt Disney and Billy Graham; they were both farmer's sons.
- Richard Burton's father was a miner.
- Samuel Goldwyn was an orphan at ten.
- Charlie Chaplin grew up in a school for destitute children.
- Frank Sinatra's father was a boxer.
- Sean Connery's father was a laborer.
- Dorothy Lamour was born in a charity ward.
- Marilyn Monroe was illegitimate.
- The fathers of Joan Crawford and Steve McQueen deserted the family home when their children were infants.

List as many of your ancestors as you can, with their place of origin and occupation.

Scene 2. **BEYOND THE FOREST**
Objective: Taking Your First "Baby Steps" into a World Outside Your Own

Get ready, it's time to venture outside your environment. Don't be afraid of expanding your horizons in the cause of expanding your personality. Most important, don't worry about what your friends think. In fact, don't even bother to consult them. It's a lot easier to become a new person with strangers; they don't have any expectations. They don't have fixed notions or preconceived ideas. Remember, no one *really* knows you but you, and that's all anyone else can know.

SCRIPT: I'm sure you go to a restaurant at least once a week. Well, even if you don't, this week you're going to go to one. I don't care which meal you choose—breakfast, lunch, dinner, or a late afternoon or midnight snack—or whether you go with someone or alone, although going with someone will make it more fun. There are but two criteria: you must choose a restaurant that you've never been to before, and it must be a restaurant that you've never been to before because you thought you didn't belong. Well, that was the old inferior you. Remember, there really is no one better! Now, don't tell me you can't afford it. You don't have to pick the most expensive restaurant in town or the most expensive item on the menu. And remember, I said you could go for any meal.

Call the restaurant well in advance of the day you are going and find out if reservations are necessary. If they are, make yours—then and there. If you plan to use your credit card, ask if they accept credit cards and which ones. If they don't, either be prepared to pay cash or choose another restaurant.

A day or two before you go, take a walk or a drive by your chosen restaurant and linger for a while. If you're in a car, it will be easier; you can just park and sit. Watch the people who are going in, noticing just one thing—how they are dressed. Is it dressy or casual? Are the women in pants or dresses? Are the men wearing suits, sport jackets, or blue jeans? Do they all have on ties? Don't let the wrong attire spoil your outing. Don't even look at what kind of car they are driving or who they are, it's not important. Remember, you have as much right to go as they do, you can mingle with whomever you please, this is a free country! Well, not quite—you will have to pay the bill.

On D-Day, if your car embarrasses you, and your chosen restaurant has valet parking, park down the street and walk the rest of the way. Don't worry, no one will notice; except maybe the valets, and what difference does that make? They are only valets.

If the restaurant is crowded and they are backed up, you might have to wait for your table. But then again, even if it's not crowded, as a first-timer you might just have to wait anyway. Maitre d's have a way of trying to "put you in your place." Don't let it bother you, it's just their way of trying to be superior. Be gracious about it, and use the wait to your advantage. Remember, you're there to broaden your horizons, not your body, so observe your surroundings: the decor, the lighting, the table arrangements—are some tables in a better spot than others? Study the other guests. Are there things about them that you admire, that you envy? A child learns by imitating his parents. Well, you're still growing up. You, too, need a role model, someone to imitate.

Okay, now you're at the table—don't be intimidated by the waiter or the captain. And when the menus arrive, if you don't understand what something is—particularly if it is in a foreign language you don't speak—then *ask*. Don't be shy. God gave you a mouth for more than eating.

Despite my world travels, I still speak, understand, and read only English. Fortunately, most ethnic restaurants in America have their menus printed in English, so ordering is not a problem. In foreign countries—well, they know I'm a tourist and they don't expect me to be able to read the menu.

French restaurants are soup of a different broth. Most of their menus, whether in New York or Memphis, are in French. If you have chosen a French restaurant and you don't speak French, just do what I do—ask them to translate it item for item. As long as you're there, you might as well eat something you like. Better yet, try something new, something you've never had and think you might like. What's the worst that could happen? You won't like it. Big deal—it's only one meal. Besides which, you're there to broaden your horizons, and you just might be pleasantly surprised and add something new to your repertoire. I'd never had fried calamari until I went to Italy, and now I can't live without them. Brussels sprouts weren't in my frame of reference until I lived in England. I tasted goose for the first time this Christmas and had never had a papaya, mango, or—can you believe—fresh pineapple before I was twenty-nine.

Now, I've set up this test early in the book, and you'll notice that I haven't told you techniques for making your entrance and your exit, or for subordinating the maitre d' and the headwaiter. Those begin in the next chapter, on overcoming inhibitions.

I'm having you do this without back-up quite deliberately. For now, just take what they dish out—in food and in the way they treat you. Remember, this is just a trial run. You may feel intimidated and insecure, but that's no big deal. Even a crab has to lie naked and vulnerable on the shore until it grows a new shell.

And believe me, you're not the only one in the restaurant to feel intimidated and pushed around. You'll profit from this test at this time, for it is a tryout of your newly discovered positive qualities. You'll gain strength from it and the courage to try again. The world is a frightening place—but it'll become less frightening as you read on, learn and adopt the tricks, gain confidence, and *progress.*

Live dangerously and experience the experience! Enjoy it, it will only make you grow. I hope just emotionally, not physically! This is only the beginning. As you begin to broaden your horizons you will broaden yourself; no pun intended. Try a new restaurant each and every time you go out, and by the time you reach Chapter Ten, "The Roar of the Restaurant and the Hush of the Crowd," you'll get an Oscar for your performance.

Go ahead, call that restaurant now.

ACT IV	**PROPS:**	**Pencil**
		Notebook
		Telephone book
		Telephone
		Library card
		Money

Scene 1. **HIGH TIME**
Objective: To Achieve Major Educational Advancement with
        Minimum Effort

Big deal, so you don't have a college degree. Neither did Burt Lancaster, Clint Eastwood, Cary Grant, Robert Mitchum, or Montgomery Clift. In fact, they didn't even have a high-school diploma.

There is no need for you ever to be embarrassed by your lack of education. It's not fixed like your roots or your "family tree." You can do something about it. If you really feel that your lack of education is holding you back, and if it really suits your style to adjust, then now is the time to do that "something" about it. The key to self-confidence is knowledge; it is our most powerful tool. There are two ways for you to build your wall of power. The first, Informal Education, is mandatory.

List the three things you find most interesting in this world besides yourself, your family, and your job:

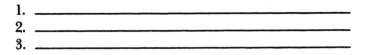

1. _____

2. _____

3. _____

Tomorrow you are to go to the library and get two books on the subject that is Number One on your list. For the next two weeks you are to spend twenty minutes a day reading. That's all, just twenty minutes, no more even if you want to. I want your frustration to come from not getting enough, not from having bitten off more than you can chew. And don't tell me you don't have time; everyone has twenty minutes. I wrote this book and another while making a record, going on promotional trips throughout England, South Africa, and Germany, discoing until dawn at least five nights a week, taking long lunches every day, and going to dinner parties almost every evening.

If, after you've finished those first two books, the subject still interests you, get some more. If, after two weeks, twenty minutes is not long enough, if it leaves you hungry, then increase your reading time. But only increase it by ten minutes a day each week. Remember, I don't want you to choke from too big a mouthful. After you've exhausted the first subject on your list, go on to the second and then the third, using the same twenty-minutes-a-day technique. If any seem boring, don't give up, don't give in right away. Give yourself the two weeks to test it. If sitting down to read is a new discipline for you, it could be it's just the discipline you're rebelling against. At the very worst, you'll have something else to talk about and less of an excuse to think about how boring you are. You might even begin to discover some of the fascinating and exciting things out there in this world.

Scene 2. THE ALL-AMERICAN CO-ED

Objective: To Complete Your Formal Education with Minimum Cost and with Minimal Interruption to Your Life

If you still feel your lack of formal education is holding you back, if your thirst for knowledge is unquenched by home reading, if you've read at least two books on each of your three listed topics, if your hungry brain is crying for more, then it's time to profit from this discovery and feed it. Now's the time to go back to school.

Neither money nor time need be a problem. There are city colleges and state universities almost everywhere that are either free or charge minimal tuition fees. Schedules that will suit almost any time frame you could desire—days, evenings, Saturdays, even Sundays. Check the yellow pages in your telephone directory or call your local Board of Education. If you've not yet gotten your high school or elementary school diploma, your Board of Education will be able to direct you to the appropriate place.

Once again, don't bite off more than you can chew. One course only the first time around. You can always increase your load next term. That school's been there a long time, it won't go anywhere. You have the rest of your life to learn and to grow; don't let your overeagerness wreck everything. If you go on overload, you'll only short-circuit.

ACT V

PROPS: **Notebook**
Pencil
Telephone
Telephone book
Mirror
Library card
Money

Scene 1. **BLOSSOMS IN THE DUST**
Objective: To See Yourself with Loving Eyes

All right, now what's bothering you, what else is holding you back? Oh, you don't like the way you look. You think you're ugly, you're fat, you're too skinny, your nose is too big, your rear end sags, your skin is pockmarked, your arms are too short. . . . Well, I'm sure all of that's true and I'm also sure that my telling you that none of it matters won't make any difference to you, because you're the one who has to look at you in the mirror. Believe me, your lack of physical perfection is not the end of the world. There is nothing about you that can't be changed—or, better still, used to your advantage.

FAVE RAVE LIST

People in My Daily Life I Consider the Most Fabulous-Looking. (They can be of either sex.)

List below your five fave raves.
1. _____
2. _____
3. _____
4. _____
5. _____

Now, before we can accentuate your positives—yes, I know it's hard to imagine anything positive about you, but believe me there is and we'll find it—we have to eliminate, or at least reduce, your negatives.

In the space below, or in your workbook, list everything physical you hate about yourself. (I'll leave you plenty of space.)

PHYSICAL HATE LIST

THE BEVERLY HILLS STYLE

You know, you're not the only one who's not perfect. In fact, some people have even taken their disadvantages and made them work for them.

Nose too big: Barbra Streisand, Danny Thomas, Jimmy Durante

Bad skin (lines and wrinkles included): Robert Redford, Richard Burton, Doris Day, Mary Tyler Moore, Tom Jones

Baldness: Burt Reynolds, Yul Brynner, Telly Savalas

Imperfect teeth: Ali McGraw, Lauren Hutton

Dodgy eyes: Karen Black, Peter Falk

Too fat: Orson Welles, Raymond Burr, Shelley Winters, Elizabeth Taylor

Too short: Richard Dreyfus, Dustin Hoffman, Madeline Kahn, Raquel Welch, Joel Grey, Mikhail Baryshnikov

Too tall: Christopher Reeve, James Stewart, Wilt Chamberlain

Bad legs: Jack Nicholson, Sally Kellerman, Donna Summer, Marcello Mastroianni

Big ears: Clark Gable, Frank Sinatra

Speech defect/peculiar accent: Humphrey Bogart, Judy Holliday, Peter Lorre, Carol Channing, Madeline Kahn

Too old: George Burns, Jack Benny, Ruth Gordon, Grandma Moses

Too hairy: Tina Turner, Elliott Gould

Too different-looking: Sissy Spacek, Glenda Jackson, Sammy Davis Jr., Phyllis Diller, Jack Palance, Bette Midler, Lily Tomlin

Mouth too large: Sophia Loren, Martha Raye, Liza Minnelli, Mick Jagger, Carly Simon, Julie Christie

Mouth too small: Shirley Maclaine, Roy Scheider

Eyes too close together: Geraldine Chaplin.

Now list everything physical that you like about yourself: *every* physical attribute you have on the plus side, including those that maybe aren't so good but also aren't so bad.

(I'm leaving a lot of space, so you'd better fill it up.)

PHYSICAL LIKE LIST

Now, rank yourself on my chart.

WOMEN

	GREAT	GOOD	FAIR
EYES	✓	✓	
GAZE	✓		✓
HAIR	✓		
TEETH	✓	✓	✓
NOSE	✓		✓
BROW	✓		
BONE STRUCTURE		✓	
COMPLEXION		✓	
BREASTS	✓	✓	
WAIST	✓		
BOTTOM	✓		
LEGS	✓		
HANDS	✓		
POSTURE	✓	✓	
AND, most important of all, EXPRESSION	✓		✓

MEN

	GREAT	GOOD	FAIR
EXPRESSION			
BEARING			
EYES			
GAZE			
HAIR			
MOUTH			
TEETH			
NOSE			
BROW			
BONE STRUCTURE			
SKIN			
SHOULDERS			
CHEST			
STOMACH			
HANDS			
LEGS			
BUTTOCKS			

No doubt you've noticed that there is no ranking below "fair" on my charts. That's because you already know what your weak points are; you've already listed them. Enough is enough—besides which, we'll be working on those a little later.

Are you surprised that you have so many strong points? It's funny, we spend so much time dwelling on the negative that it becomes all we can see. When you focus on something, that's all that exists. Now that you are aware of your strong points, you can begin to focus on them. You can begin to perpetuate the positive.

Scene 2. **LITTLE ISLES OF FREEDOM**
Objective: Simple Techniques to Apply for a More Physically Perfect You

I'm sure you'll find that as your sense of self and power develops,

43

so will your physical sense. So, until that Self has fully blossomed, we're not going to do anything too dramatic. Believe me, there's plenty of time, besides which you'll need that time to save your money. Any dramatic alterations, anything requiring surgery (there is *nothing* that the knife can't change; see Chapter Five) will be costly. For now, let's just see if we can spruce you up a bit.

SCRIPT:

1. **If you're fat, go on a diet.** Now, not tomorrow. There is a wide range to choose from, and *any* diet will work if you stick to it. I happen to think mine, The Beverly Hills Diet, is the best. After all, it is the cure for fat! You can eat everything and anything, you don't have to weigh or measure your foods, you don't have to count calories, and it is a plan that you can adapt to your lifestyle. But this isn't a plug for my book. If it works for you, fine. If not, God knows there are shelves of diet books to choose from. Go to the bookstore, look through all of them, and pick the one that suits you best. Then stick to it! Always remember, all the food you think you will be missing out on will still be there tomorrow. Nothing's leaving the planet!

2. **Get a new hairstyle.** Unless, of course, you *really* love your present one. There's only one stipulation: you must go to someone new, someone who doesn't know you, someone who has never seen you before. Someone who can look at you with a whole new perspective, with no preconceived idea of who or what you are. Someone who will look at you with new eyes and give you a whole new look. If you don't know who to go to, check with one of your fave raves, preferably your number-one favorite, and go to whoever he or she uses.

   Or change the color. According to international hair colorist Nicholas Modlin, of Gerard Bollei in Manhattan—whose clients have included a Mommy Dearest, a Number 10 actress, a princess who wears wooden shoes, an ever-changing blonde-sometimes-redhead English male pop star—"a change in hair color is like a change in life. Drab, dull people almost always have drab, dull hair. When you add vibrance and color to their hair, the same thing happens to their personalities." Yes, it's true—blondes do have more fun. Both of us (Nicholas and I) can vouch for that!

3. **Out of shape (not fat—that requires diet), just sort of soft and flabby, a little paunchy?** Well, start exercising. There is a plethora of organized and disorganized activities to choose from: walking, aerobics, gymnastics, dance, jogging. Pick up those rusty golf clubs, get out that age-rotted tennis racket. Just get off your duff and do something—anything. However, do not begin exercising if you have just begun a diet. It's just too much discipline all at once. Remember, I don't want you to go on overload and short-circuit. Once you have been on your diet for two weeks, then and only then may you begin to exercise.

One more restriction: when you begin an exercise program, you are not to exercise for more than fifteen minutes per day for the first week. You may then increase the time by fifteen minutes, but you may not go beyond thirty minutes for at least three more weeks. From that point on, let your energy be your guide. I repeat, do not bite off more than you can chew, or you'll choke. All too often, in our desperate attempt toward self-improvement, we set up unrealistic expectations for ourselves, and they only serve to undermine us. We just rebel under the pressure. Well, haven't you?

4. **Go to the movies and think about more than the story.** Look at the actors, think about the other films you have seen them in. Mentally begin to compare their different roles. Watch them, study them, be aware of the parts they're playing. Because, you see, that's what you're doing, too; you're playing a part, only your audience and your stage will be bigger—it's the world!

5. **Get fashion magazines.** Yes, all of you—men and women. *Vogue, Harper's Bazaar, Esquire, Gentleman's Quarterly, W., M.* If you can't afford to buy them, browse through them at a magazine rack or at the library. Become aware of how the really "beautiful" people look—their aura, their sense of self. Study them, see what techniques of theirs you can adopt and adapt.

6. **Not for women only.** Makeup can create miracles; some of the most beautiful people in the world are horrors without it. Go to a makeup artist and put your face in the artist's hands. Don't

rebel when you see the results; remember, it's a whole new look, a look you just might have to get used to. So give yourself time before you wash it off. Start using the techniques you learned— well, at least start practicing them. If you can't afford a makeup artist, get a book. *The Way Bandy Makeup Book* will teach you everything you need to know—if you practice, that is. You probably won't do very well in the beginning, but then, if you were handy with makeup, you'd already be using it to its fullest potential.

(For a Beverly Hills Style Home Makeup Consultation, see p. 263)

Just one last scene—a kind of dress rehearsal before we actually start filming.

Scene 3. MOURNING BECOMES ELECTRA
Objective: To Remove Your Shroud and Let Your Excellence
Blaze Forth

Go back to Act I, Scene 3, to your "All the Things I Am" list (page 28) and in sentence form list all the words you underlined. Then go to Act V, Scene 1, to your *Physical Like List* (page 41), do the same, and create an "I'm My Everything, Everything I Love" list.

It might look something like this: Creative and thoughtful. Sympathetic and understanding. Great expression, good teeth. Good breasts and posture.

Well kid, that's you. Not as bad as you thought—right? In fact, you're GREAT!

Now it's time to start taking all those wonderful things that are wonderfully you and put them to use. Let's get on with the rehearsal; it's time you started living.

CAUTION: I'm not telling you not to read the rest of this book.— *au contraire*—I want you to see the fun and glamour that's out there waiting for you. But you are not—I repeat, you are not—to go to any other section and do any of the other scenes until you have completed every scene in this chapter. If you haven't established your most positive identity, you will only fail. It won't be any fun, and you'll only be the loser. Be patient and you'll succeed. Come on, isn't it time you started winning?

I'M MY EVERYTHING, EVERYTHING I LOVE LIST

3

Stage Fright
(Overcoming Inhibitions)

ACT I   **PROPS:** Pencil

It's great now that you're beginning to know and improve on who and what you are; and it's even better now that you're finally beginning to appreciate and esteem your own special qualities. But there's still something holding you back. And it's the something that's always held you back. *You!*

You've been your own worst enemy, the biggest obstacle in your life. You and your inhibitions—your feelings of inferiority, your fear of rejection, your fear of being laughed at, your fear of failure. You're even afraid of success.

Well, the time has come to shed your shroud of inhibitions. It's time to fling your arms open wide and blaze forth into a brave new world.

It should come as some consolation to you to know that you're not the only one who's inhibited. We've all had to learn to let go at one time or another, even the people we'd least suspect . . .

At an Oscar party I went to some years ago, given by Grace (Mrs. Harold) Robbins, a famous director-turned-author was talking about one of the nominees, whom he had directed in her first role.

After three hours of nothing—nothing, that is, but frustration—he "stopped tape" and called a break. She could've been a wooden Indian. He called her aside and, using every four-letter word in most of our vocabularies, began hurling abusive insults at her.

Insults not about her acting but about her, personally. He concluded his tirade with:

"And I wouldn't sleep with you if you were the last woman on earth and you begged me."

He turned on his heels and walked away. Her body became rigid. Then, shaking, she began to scream and throw things at him, matching him obscenity for obscenity.

He turned back to her. "You bitch, I've got all that on tape, so now that I've seen you do it, get the hell out there and act!" Although she didn't win the Oscar the night I heard that story, she has won several since.

P.S. No one is totally uninhibited. If they are, they're probably locked up.

Feelings of inferiority should no longer be a *major* issue. By rehearsing the scenes in chapter two, you've started taking control of your life. You're looking good and getting better. You're bright, shining, energetic; and you've got a lot to talk about. Can you even imagine you'd gone so long without reading? Isn't it fun being able to participate, not just sit there like a dummy with nothing to say? What could you possibly still feel inferior about? Oh, that you're not perfect? Come on, Rome wasn't built in a day!

What, you haven't been rehearsing the scenes in chapter two? You think they're silly, and you're embarrassed? No, you're the one that's silly because, if you don't do them, this book won't do you any good. I've said it before, but I'll say it again: *you must do The Beverly Hills Style for it to become you.* If some of the scenes have embarrassed you or made you uncomfortable, they are probably the most important ones for your development. It's your embarrassment that we need to conquer. By doing the scenes, you'll get over it.

You must stop feeling physically inferior, so if you have not yet done the scenes in chapter two, go back and do them now, before you go on.

Coping with rejection is one of the hardest things we have to deal with in life, and yet we experience it many times over in the course of the day. Rejection is the most common negative interaction between human beings. Everyone is privy to it, everyone is affected by it: no one likes it, and everyone fears it—including the superstars. . . .

I was having dinner in Rome with Roger Moore, Mel Brooks, and Monica Vitti. With an all-star cast like that, it wasn't without reason that our dinner table was constantly besieged by other diners in the restaurant requesting autographs. I turned to Roger and asked him if it wasn't a big nuisance, wasn't it making him crazy? He'd barely eaten a bit of dinner—every time he picked up his fork it was replaced with a pen. He finished signing an autograph and turned to me, smiling,

"Judy, when they stop asking, then it'll make me crazy."

> **Rejection:** 1. to refuse to acknowledge or submit to
> 2. to refuse to take or accept
> 3. to refuse to grant, consider or accede to
> 4. to throw out as useless or unsatisfactory
> *The Merriam Webster Dictionary*

Though we're inclined to think of rejection as something personal, someone not liking or wanting us, it goes beyond that. Though often disguised as something else, it exists on every level of human relations. It's not only the lover casting you aside; it's the stranger on the elevator who looks through you when you smile at him or her. It's the shop clerk who waits on someone else before you, or the telephone information operator who refused to look a little harder for that number. Rejection is not getting the job you should have, the promotion you deserved, the hug you wanted, or the positive support, encouragement, and love you needed. Rejection is not getting anything you want, expect, deserve, or need from anyone or anything. That's right, even inanimate objects can reject you. For instance, when your scale doesn't go down regardless of how good you've been on your diet, that's rejection.

You're not even aware of most rejection. It happens so often that it just slips by unnoticed. In fact, you're not even responsible for most of it, nor is it even you that's being rejected—you just happen to be the scapegoat for the other person, the rejecter.

If you recognize and acknowledge rejection and learn to accept and use it, your awareness will minimize the occurrences. While you may not have control over another person's feelings and reactions and may be unable to make all rejection disappear, the new-found strength you're developing will help lessen its effect on you.

Rejection from strangers is easy to slough off. Since there's nothing personal about it, it can't really hurt. However, as inconsequential as it seems, it's important that you deal with it and turn it around. Each time you turn a rejection into an acceptance, it's a pat on the back. Don't think anyone can get too many of those.

Scene 1. **BRIEF ENCOUNTER**
Objective: To Improve Your Interactions with, and Overcome Your Fear of Rejection from, Strangers

For the next week you are going to approach three strangers a day. From the first you'll seek directions. To the second (someone you've selected because of something obvious like an item of clothing or perfume that you find attractive, etc.), you'll give a compliment. And from the third stranger you are to ask the time. You can approach your strangers any time you find yourself in close proximity to one—on an elevator, in the subway, or just walking down the street.

Keep in mind that in every interaction, there is an action and a reaction. If the majority of people you approach are hostile, uptight, uncooperative, or unresponsive, then perhaps it's *you*, and a reaction that you're creating. Be aware, and if you find this happening check yourself against the following Positive-Response-Creating checklist. You should be able to answer yes to all of the questions. After each stranger interaction, fill out a Stranger-Interaction Barometer.

POSITIVE-RESPONSE-CREATING CHECKLIST

1. I was courteous. I said "excuse me," "please," and "thank you" when appropriate.
2. My body language said, "I won't hurt you."
3. I made eye contact.
4. I smiled.

STRANGER-INTERACTION BAROMETER

THE ASKING DIRECTIONS FROM, STRANGER
(Fill in blanks, or check where appropriate.)

Where Asked	Time	Male (✔)	Female (✔)	Approx Age	Positive Resp (✔)	Negative Resp (✔)
1.						
2.						
3.						
4.						
5.						
6.						
7.						

Where Asked	Time	Male (✔)	Female (✔)	Approx Age	Positive Resp (✔)	Negative Resp (✔)
1.						
2.						
3.						
4.						
5.						
6.						
7.						

Where Asked	Time	Male (✔)	Female (✔)	Approx Age	Positive Resp (✔)	Negative Resp (✔)
1.						
2.						
3.						
4.						
5.						
6.						
7.						

THE GIVING COMPLIMENT TO STRANGER
(Fill in blanks, or check where appropriate.)

Compliment Given	Where Given	Time	Approx Age	Positive Resp (✔)	Negative Resp (✔)	No Resp	Reply
1.							
2.							
3.							
4.							
5.							
6.							
7.							

Compliment Given	Where Given	Time	Approx Age	Positive Resp (✔)	Negative Resp (✔)	No Resp	Reply
1.							
2.							
3.							
4.							
5.							
6.							
7.							

Compliment Given	Where Given	Time	Approx Age	Positive Resp (✔)	Negative Resp (✔)	No Resp	Reply
1.							
2.							
3.							
4.							
5.							
6.							
7.							

Isn't it interesting how difficult it is for some people to accept compliments, to accept hearing something nice about themselves. Somehow they have a way of making you feel so wrong, or so stupid. Is it any wonder that compliments are so difficult to give?

"WHAT TIME IS IT, PLEASE," STRANGER
(Fill in blanks, or check where appropriate.)

Where Asked	Time	Male (✔)	Female (✔)	Approx Age	Positive Resp (✔)	Negative Resp (✔)
1.						
2.						
3.						
4.						
5.						
6.						
7.						

Where Asked	Time	Male (✔)	Female (✔)	Approx Age	Positive Resp (✔)	Negative Resp (✔)
1.						
2.						
3.						
4.						
5.						
6.						
7.						

Where Asked	Time	Male (✔)	Female (✔)	Approx Age	Positive Resp (✔)	Negative Resp (✔)
1.						
2.						
3.						
4.						
5.						
6.						
7.						

Now it's time to assess yourself, to add up your score. Count the number of positive responses and the number of negative responses. If the positives outnumber the negatives, you've gotten the message: now you can only get better, stronger, less fearful of and more adept at interacting with strangers. Continue your rehearsals with three strangers a day for the next month.

If your negative responses outnumber your positive responses, we've got a problem. If could simply be your judgment of character. If you're not yet a very good judge of character, this is something to be aware of when you try again. You must get this right, or there's absolutely no point in going further.

But before you re-rehearse the scene, go over your Stranger-

Interaction Barometer and see if there's another category, other than negative response, with many similarities: Maybe age is a factor. Was everyone you selected about the same age? You'll often find one age group more uptight than another. Did you ask more members of one sex than the other? Please, next time keep them equal. What about *when* you approached them; time often has a strong effect on people's moods and their interactions with someone else, especially a stranger.

You'll see, you'll be more successful the second time. You'll handle yourself much better, and it will be a lot easier. You've learned from your mistakes, your judgment of people will be better, and you'll be more self-assured.

Go over your Positive-Response-Creating checklist: does your smile come easily and naturally; is it honest and candid? No one's eyes are going to burn a hole through you, so look at them—make eye contact. Words like "please" and "thank you" don't cost a cent, and you'll probably be paid back with a smile. So come on, just go ahead and do it. I promise you, nobody's going to bite you. Wasn't your best friend once a stranger?

Oh, a little P.S. Don't expect every stranger to be "super-nice" back to you, no matter how terrifically you're playing your part. Regardless of how positive *your* action, some people—in fact, most people—are so into themselves, they just aren't even aware of you or how they're relating to you. Just take a bow for your performance and don't take their reactions personally. Instead, feel pity for them for their self-absorption.

A little hint: Next time, look before you leap. Before you approach someone, stop for a moment and study him or her. Let your natural instincts go to work. They should tell you who's going to be nasty and who's going to be nice.

Social Rejection is probably the most personal of all rejections and is done by people who, unlike our current friends and our families, don't really know us—the new people in our lives who have no expectations of us and no preconceived ideas of who or what we are. Whether it's romancing or meeting potential new friends, this is when our *self* and our hearts are really on the line.

THE BEVERLY HILLS STYLE

People either accept us or they don't. They either want to be our friends or our lovers or they don't. They either like us or they don't. Or so it seems.

But the truth is that Social Rejection is not unlike other forms of rejection: most of the time the rejection has nothing to do with you; it is usually based on whatever is going on in the rejecters' lives at the moment. They probably don't even realize that they're rejecting you or that you want to be friends with them.

Everyone is insecure in some way. Some people just wear better disguises than others—disguises that give the impression that they have their acts together . . .

Some years ago I went to group therapy for a few months. The night of the first meeting we all arrived a bit earlier than necessary and stood around the waiting room eyeing each other nervously. I had arrived *very* early and had tucked myself inconspicuously into a chair in the corner. Most of the others looked so together, I wondered why they were there. Once the session began and we all started to bare our souls, I realized that even the most together-looking of them all was as neurotic and insecure as I; they had all just donned costumes and masks and were playing award-winning roles.

Believe me, as unique as we all may be, the fear of rejection is something we all share, even those in the limelight. There aren't *any of us* who don't feel a twinge of pain when someone turns the other way or when no one notices us. . .

A gentleman friend of mine recently had dinner with my "dream man." (My dream man—the vision of his icy blue eyes has probably sent millions of other women off to slumberland as well.) It's hard to imagine that this actor-turned-director could possibly be concerned about going unnoticed, and yet when my friend asked the restaurant manager to remove a pesky photographer he was told that it couldn't be done; the photographer had been hired by his dinner companion.

Social rejection strikes from all angles. Have you ever moved into a new neighborhood and sat waiting for people to coffee-klatch with you? Joined a tennis club and found the backboard your only partner?

How many times have you started a new job and found everyone in the lunchroom staring at you as you sat alone in the corner eating your bologna on white with mayo, drowning your sorrows and loneliness in your diet cola? What about the country club you've been wanting to join, the bridge club you've been trying to get into, or the softball team at the park you'd like to play first base with? Nobody's breaking down your door—nobody's standing waiting for you, arms wide open.

Believe me, it's not just you.

They aren't *waiting* for anyone! The only way an interaction is ever going to happen is if you make it happen. You've got to get out on the ice if you ever expect to break it. Keep in mind, however, that we're talking about people who are omnipresent in your life, people you certainly don't want to alienate. Since you don't know how thin the ice is, a bit of caution is suggested. Skate slowly at first—if you break your leg, it will only slow you down.

Scene 2. BREAKING THE ICE
Objective: Making Friends out of Strangers

How many of your neighbors do you already know? How many do you want to know? No one? Come on, there's got to be one or two you don't already know, who look as if they might be valuable additions to your repertoire of friends and acquaintances.

We live in dangerous times, and people are wary of strangers knocking on their doors. The only time it's permissible to ring someone's doorbell to make contact is if you are brand spanking new to a neighborhood and live in a house or community where the dwellings are widely separated and day-to-day contact is rare. If you live in an apartment-type situation or a neighborhood where the houses are close together, you must wait for an "accidental" encounter.

The next time you find yourself in close proximity with a neighbor, why not try giving him or her a compliment? That should be easy for you, and you know what an excellent icebreaker it is. Better yet, ask for advice. All of us love being needed, and always think "ours" is "the best" and are anxious to share it. "What dry cleaner do you use?" Or, if you've been in the neighborhood for a while, rephrase your question: "I've been having so much trouble with dry cleaners, which one do you use?"

Auto mechanics, unless you live in a metropolitan area where few people have cars, are another common denominator among people and a particularly good opening gambit for men. Simply substitute garage or mechanic for dry cleaner.

Pet owners love talking about their pets, and their veterinarian is the "only one!" This time substitute vet for dry cleaner, or if you don't have a pet you can say, "I've been thinking about getting a dog (or cat or a parakeet—whatever), and don't know any veterinarians—who do you use?"

If you have children, pediatricians are a hot topic.

Make your neighborhood a playground instead of a war zone, and it will be so much fun to come home.

Oftentimes, what we construe as rejection is really other people's inability to accept what we want to give them. This is *their* emotional deficiency and, once again, has nothing to do with us. It's easy to understand a negative reaction when we're being obnoxious, hostile, or argumentative, but when we're being loving or affectionate, and someone turns away from us, we get confused— we didn't do anything, yet we're being rejected, so we must have done something. We never stop to consider that it's *their* hands that are tied behind their backs and that they're simply incapable of grasping ours as we hold ours out to them. If you watch for it, you'll be prepared, and if it happens it won't hurt you or cause you pain. Instead, you should feel sympathy for them. They're the ones who are missing out on one of life's great pleasures: YOU!

Scene 3. LOVE AND WAR
Objective: To Reinforce the Bond of Love with the People You
Care Most About

Those same five "most important people in your life" are going
to play one very important last scene with you. As always, it is best
to communicate with them in person, but if face-to-face contact
still embarrasses you, the telephone is an acceptable second choice.
Letters are at the very bottom of the list and should only be used if
in-person or telephone communication is impossible.

There is going to be one major difference in your procedure this
time: your proclamation is the reason for the conversation, the
meeting was created so you could make it. Get right to the point
without preliminaries or explanations. Look them straight in the
eye, smile, and say, "I just wanted to let you know how important
you are to me. Thank you for being so honest."

Don't run away, you're not quite finished. Besides, your knees
are probably knocking too much for you to get very far. Smile at
them for a couple of seconds and, if you can, give them a hug. If
showing affection has been difficult for you, this would be a good
time to break through that barrier. If you can't, well, that's all right,
too; I'm not going to force your hand, make you the "star" when
you still need more time as an understudy. I don't want you to get
stage fright and drop out of the theater. Who would be my star?
After all, you are the lead in this show.

After each proclamation, fill out a "What Can I say, Dear, After
I've Said I Love You" proclamation (see example on the following
page).

MY "WHAT CAN I SAY, DEAR, AFTER I'VE SAID I LOVE YOU" PROCLAMATION

NAME:
RELATIONSHIP:
HIS/HER RESPONSE TO MY PROCLAMATION:
POSITIVE — ACCEPTED IT
NEGATIVE — REJECTED IT
I WAS / I WASN'T SURPRISED (cross out nonapplicable)
I WAS / I WASN'T DISAPPOINTED (cross out nonapplicable)
I DID / I DIDN'T HUG HIM/HER (cross out nonapplicable)
IF DID NOT, WHY NOT:

_____

_____

_____

Once you have made your proclamation, and, I hope, physically expressed your affection, it is most important that you terminate the conversation and disengage yourself immediately. Most probably, your friend will want to turn your proclamation into a major discussion, which, at this point, could confuse the issue and you as well. If the friend begins to discuss it before you get away, just smile and say, "Please, I *really have nothing* more to say, and I'd prefer not to discuss it any further." Smile again and look at them with pleading eyes (you shouldn't have to do anything to attain "pleading eyes" if you're truly playing your part—that is, if you're really doing what you should be doing—your emotion of the moment will convey this). Stand your ground. Don't let your friend or your relationship intimidate you into giving in.

Dash off to a quiet place as soon as you can, so you can fill in your workbook. Delight in the love that fills your heart, that's lit your eyes and put that smile on your face. Go look in the mirror—can you see how much you've grown, how much taller you are? Notice how much higher you're holding your head.

You have so much to give, how can anyone possibly ever reject you?

P.S. Wait until you see how much easier it is all going to be now.

ACT II

PROPS: Pencil
Paint or crayon
Paper

How do you think Jackie Onassis felt when a rather gross magazine made a calendar from photos taken of her sunbathing nude?

No one wants to be laughed at. No one enjoys being the object of ridicule.

> **Ridicule:** to laugh at or make fun of contemptuously
> **Contempt:** the act of despising

The fear of ridicule, of being laughed at, is probably a greater cause of inhibition than the fear of rejection. Sure, "no man is an island," but there are instances—and this happens to be one of them—in which we carry it to the extreme. We live our lives based on, and worried about, what other people think of us. What we don't seem to realize is that other people don't think. At least not about us! Ultimately we all put ourselves first. It's called self-preservation. We are all far too self-absorbed to be really affected by another person's actions. Well, aren't you the center of your universe? Aren't most of your thoughts, at least the thoughts that affect you, about you? With this and the definition of ridicule in mind, what do you think you could possibly do that could affect another person strongly enough to provoke ridicule? How many people actually provoke you to that degree? Quite frankly, you aren't important enough to anyone else to really affect them. Well, at least not on the level that we're talking about here.

Scene 1. **THE HORSE WITH THE FLYING TAIL**
Objective: To See That Nothing You Do Could Be Ridiculous Enough to Provoke Someone Else's Ridicule

On the "Let Me Tell You What a Jerk I Am" page that follows

(or in your workbook), I want you to list all the dumb things you do that you think someone else would laugh at. As you can see, you have a whole page and no numbers—I don't want to set up any parameters or give you any idea of how many things there should be. After all, if you just use your imagination, I'm sure you'll be able to conjure up a plethora of causes for ridicule.

LET ME TELL YOU WHAT A JERK I AM

Is your imagination exhausted? Have you thought of every possible way in which you could make a fool of yourself?

Now, go through your list, imagining that you are observing other people doing the things you've listed. Would you laugh at them? If you can answer yes, then take it one step further. Would you be laughing at them, or with them? The difference: if the act provokes your amusement, it's with them; if it provokes your contempt, it's at them. Now, really, if you observed another human being doing any act on that list, would it affect you so strongly that you would really respond with contempt? Of course not, you jerk!

Oh, and as far as those embarrassing moments go—believe me, no one is immune. We've all felt like or made fools of ourselves at one time or another and lived through it.

How do you think Richard Nixon felt when he got caught?

or

What about Jay Bernstein, Farrah Fawcett's, and Suzanne Sommer's mentor? To be fired by both of them simultaneously—the gossip columns had a field day.

All of us, even the most pragmatic among us, have a spark of creativity. Developing and using that creativity can be a constant source of nourishment and an effective means of escape. What we seem to forget is that creative expression can be used solely for our personal enjoyment. And unfortunately, as in everything else we do, we allow what we think other people will think of us to inhibit us. We judge the product of our creative expression by how we think others will judge it, and more often than not, we don't even give it, or them, a chance.

Creative appreciation is subjective. Your creative expression is an expression of you, so how can *you* possibly view it objectively?

Particularly if expressing yourself creatively is something new for you. Then it's more difficult to be objective—you're even more insecure about it, more critical. And because you think it's terrible, you automatically assume everyone else will agree. So, without showing it to anyone, or without any feedback, you hide or destroy it and stifle your *Self.*

Or perhaps you do take a chance; you do show it to someone whose opinion you value, and that person has a negative reaction. That's it. You go no further. One negative opinion is all it takes. There's no point in asking anyone else; why make an even bigger fool out of yourself? What a jerk you were to think that you could paint or write or sing? It'll be a long time before you ever pick up that brush, or that pen, or open your mouth again—if ever!

That's the way I was. I never thought I could write. I never even kept a diary because it sounded so stupid when I'd reread it. My first somewhat serious attempt at writing was for a public relations expert who needed my biography to help me promote my Beverly Hills Diet Center. After I wrote it, I thought it was terrible—very trite, and *very* boring. But when I read it to her she roared with laughter. This expression of her enjoyment, which at first made me cringe—I thought she was laughing at me—became my source of inspiration. Three years later, *The Beverly Hills Diet,* the best-selling book of 1981, was born.

Scene 2. **ART IS**
Objective: To Acknowledge the Creative You

Read the following poem to three people, either in person or on the telephone. This can be any three people in your daily life, including your Big Five. When you approach them, simply say, "I've written a poem and I'm going to enter it in a contest. I'd like your opinion." Begin reading the poem immediately. When you finish, look them straight in the eye, smile, and say, "Well, what do you think?"

Try to keep a straight face, and by all means don't laugh. (You certainly wouldn't want them to think you're trying to make a fool out of them, would you?) *Listen* to what they have to say. Don't comment, just nod your head, say thank you, and make a quick getaway. Then you can laugh.

IN EMPATHY WITH A ROSE
A Poem

I saw a lone rose
Growing out in space
It reminded me of the blush
On a girl's face
I thought of a time
When you were mine
When the world was young
And life was fine
But that was long ago
Now my heart's turned to stone
That solitary rose, made me feel so alone.

After you've read my poem to three people you are to write one of your own and then read it to three other people. (Come on, you lived through the first three, didn't you?) Let's tap into your creativity and put it to the test. Let's see if there's any gold in them thar hills.

After you've done the poem I want you either to paint or to draw something and then test it on three other people. Trust me, if you keep exploring, you will find that gold . . . your expression of YOU.

Most of the popular shows on television are situation comedies, and many of our most popular television personalities are comedians: shows and people looking at the lighter side of life, with smiles on their faces. Do you remember all those great old Gene Kelly musicals, films that turned everything into a song-and-dance routine and viewed life through rose-colored spectacles? Fun, weren't they?

Often the stress of day-to-day living closes us off from the fun in life and robs us of our sense of humor. Getting too caught up in the serious side of life is like being caught up in a rip tide; it begins to drag you down and drown you. Come on, let's put a little of that fun back into your life; in fact, let's go get silly! And, if you're worried about people thinking that you're crazy, just remember: THEY DON'T THINK.

Scene 3. **THE HUMAN COMEDY**
Objective: To Become Free Enough to Do Whatever You Want to Do Regardless of What Other People Think

Okay, Gene (Kelly), or should I call you Jane (Powell), you're about to turn your life into a musical comedy. Pick a street, anywhere in your own neighborhood or on the other side of town, and walk down the entire length of the block singing a song. If you happen to know "On the Street Where You Live," what could be better? If not, do any song you know well. You don't have to belt it out unless you want to, but it must be audible. The louder, the better. The more foolish you feel, the more attention you'll get. Or, as you'll soon see, not get. Well, maybe you'll raise a few eyebrows and get a few sidewise glances. Some people might even stop and look at you for a moment, but a moment will be the extent of their attention. And believe me, they'll forget you in less time.

Trust me. You can't really start living until you can make life fun; and when you see that you can get through this scene without "dying," get ready, because your life has finally begun.

P.S. If you live in a small town and you're worried that you'll be labeled the town nut, remember if the town is that small they already know it if you are or not—a nut, that is—and I doubt if this will change any minds.

ACT III
SUCCESS AND FAILURE

Following her award-winning performance in *The Three Faces of Eve*, Joanne Woodward had, to quote *Variety*, "Six flops. Her seventh attempt won critical acclaim."

Failure didn't stop Regis Philbin, charismatic host of "The Morning Show" and "Regis Philbin's Lifestyle." Ousted after many years as co-host of "A.M. Los Angeles," it was quite some time before he reappeared in the limelight. He didn't allow failure to be his defeat—instead, he used it as his springboard to reach new heights of success.

Stefan Edberg, John McEnroe's Swedish opponent in the 1984 U.S. Open, didn't let the inevitablility of failure stop him. . . . "I learned a lot. I have a lot to improve. . . . I had seen McEnroe play and had an idea how to play him. But it didn't work out. I didn't have a chance at all."

Elizabeth Taylor had eight Oscar nominations before she finally won the best actress award for *Butterfield 8*.

It's a good thing Robin Williams didn't take his college classmates and their prediction seriously; they voted him the least likely to succeed.

For every success there are uncountable failures. Failures, rather than being feared, should be welcomed—they are experiences from which you can learn and grow. With each failure comes the added strength that can only serve to make you stand a little taller, a little straighter, and a little stronger.

Sure, failure hurts. You'd be abnormal not to feel terrible when you don't achieve something that you've worked hard at attaining, something that's important to you. And if you don't allow yourself to feel the pain and disappointment failure leaves, you're not being honest with yourself; if you deny or ignore it when it happens, you'll never profit from the experience and you'll just make the same mistake all over again.

It's your fear of failure that's the largest stumbling block on the road to success. It's stopping you from trying. Always remember you are your own worst enemy. Fear is inhibiting all your aspirations and dreams, and without dreams what have you got to come true? All you'll ever have is just what you have today. Are you satisfied with that?

So stop hiding in the wings. Jump onto that stage when the curtain goes up, and dare to take another chance. Whatever the outcome, you will have succeeded. You'll always come out ahead. If you should experience a failure, if you should occasionally be a loser, the knowledge you gain from the experiences is what will ultimately turn you into a winner!

Success is often far more dangerous than failure. If you fear it, or abuse it, it can destroy you.

> "Once a person starts to get famous the very thing he needs to remain extraordinary starts to fall away; that is equalitarian relationships. Instead you get an entourage and they will tell you whatever you want to hear. . . ."
> —Talia Shire talking about her brother, producer/director, Francis Ford Coppola (*The Godfather, Apocalypse Now*).

Success carries with it a responsibility, the responsibility of living up to the image that success represents. When you're a star, when you're Number One, you must act the part; it's expected of you. Yet at the same time you're damned for your "attitude." Damned if you do, damned if you don't. The people around you fall into two camps: either they pridefully share in your joy or they fold their arms across their chests waiting for the "inevitable," gloating as you fall. Farrah Fawcett saw it happen: "they" built her into a superstar and then almost succeeded in tearing her down.

The most devastating aspect of success is the pressure of maintaining the achievement. It becomes overwhelming, and oftentimes self-defeating. Jane Pauley had this to say about her own success: "Sometimes I become a slave to paranoia. . . . Everyone wants my job and I want to hold on to it."

When the fear of not being able to maintain success takes over, we begin to lose our sense of naiveté, that part of us that took chances. When success itself becomes more important than the act of achievement, it quickly slips from the grasp and is gone before it can be recaptured.

Saturday Night Fever was the rage of the world, it shot John Travolta to the top. His next few ventures, unfortunately, were not as successful. It must have been devastating. On the set of *Urban Cowboy*, he spoke to a friend: "My success as an actor depends on this movie. I can't survive another flop like *Moment to Moment*. If this one's not a hit, I'm going to give it all up!"

The sweet smell of success is more costly than the finest French perfume. Value it.

There is no special scene in this act. You're already playing it: a scene where every second, every action, can be measured in terms of failure or success. It's a scene, however, that you're not just acting out; you're living it every day. Become your own success, and your success will become you.

ENCORE

Go up to four strangers, random strangers with whom you find yourself in close proximity, and repeat the following: "I used to be shy. I'm not shy anymore, and I'll never be shy again." An elevator is a particularly good place for this one. If you're lucky, the elevator door will open as you say your last sentence and you'll be able to walk out without anyone seeing the flush on your face. Not from embarrassment, of course—from the heat of success.

Then take your bow, and the curtain will come down.

4

Go for It!

ACT I   **PROPS: Pencil**
               Money
               Vehicle of
                  transportation

They came into this world naked, and now they're sporting minks and diamonds. . . .

Trust me, it just didn't happen! You better believe they wore polyester in between.

From nobody to the most wanted . . .

Instant stardom—it's a myth.

Do you really think that Lana Turner just walked into Schwab's Drugstore on Sunset Boulevard in Hollywood, sat on a stool, and was discovered?

Samuel Goldwyn didn't just become the head of a major motion picture studio; he'd swept floors in a factory when he was ten.

Do you think that the president of IBM goes to work at nine and leaves at five? Do you think he worries about weekends off and leisure time?

Steve McQueen didn't just drop into Hollywood a star. He knew what hard work and struggling were all about. He'd been a merchant seaman, a docker, a bartender, a salesman, a bookie's runner, a beachboy, and a TV repairman.

Ask Robert Mitchum about paying dues. He dug ditches, worked in a coal mine and a factory, wrote songs, clerked in a shoe shop, and had, you'll pardon the pun, twenty-seven professional boxing matches under or is it below his belt, before he got his first job as an actor.

Success! Stardom!

No one handed it to them on a silver platter. It didn't just happen. They *made* it happen.

They had GO POWER. They were goal-oriented—they were one-sighted about what they wanted. They used their DFC—Dedication, Focus, and Concentration. They were dedicated to excellence—they knew they had to be the best and they really worked to achieve it.

They focused on their goal, and they concentrated to achieve it.

Everything they did, all their energy was directed toward that one thing—getting what they wanted . . .

"From the time I was ten years old, I wanted to be the best in something." Arnold Schwarzenegger talks about the early years. "Even when I was that age, I would daydream about leaving Austria and coming to America." What he wanted to be the best in, he decided, was bodybuilding, which he discovered when, at fifteen, he began lifting weights to develop his legs for soccer. "Once I decided I wanted to do it, I learned about the body, how it works, how each muscle can be worked. I felt like Leonardo da Vinci, I was a sculptor shaping the body." Soon he dropped out of other sports to devote his full attention to his new-found interest, training six days a week and continuously increasing the weight he lifted and the length of his training sessions. He poured over American magazines like *Muscle Builder* and *Mr. America* and assiduously followed the adventure films of strong-man actors—Steve Reeves, Gordon Mitchell, Brad Harris, Steve Forrest, and above all, Greg Park. His parents, alarmed at his obsession, forbade him to spend more than three nights a week at the gym. To circumvent their curfew, he set up his own gym in an unheated room at home, where he trained even on the coldest days in the winter, when the temperature dropped below zero.

The story continues, but you've seen the result.

Success! Achievement! The ultimate validation of your sense of purpose, the ultimate validation of your sense of self. Getting what you want—the brass ring on the merry-go-round. If all those stars could get what they wanted by making it happen, so will you once you know how. Believe me, you have the potential, we all do. We all have Go Power. We all have DFC. You just have to learn how to use yours, how to control and direct it. Soon you won't even have to grab for the ring, it will fall into your hand. Your will and determination, your focus and your concentration will see to that.

Winners strive for winning: it is the fuel that feeds them, the staff of life. You too must go after what you want with the utmost concentration of purpose.

"I do exactly what I'm supposed to do. . . . I get on the court and off as fast as I can, I work on my concentration. . . . They, the fans, enjoy seeing someone go out and give their guts to win. You can't fool these people. You can't beg for their support. You've got to earn it. . . ."—Tennis champ Jimmy Connors.

Success doesn't apply only to the "big things" like getting a better job or making a million dollars. Every minute of your life, each one of your acts, is measured in terms of your success or your failure, getting what you want or not getting what you want. Take that simple act of asking a stranger for the time. If you didn't walk away from that interaction knowing the time, you didn't get what you wanted. If you were one of the many that had to continue rehearsing that scene because of too many negative responses, I'm sure you discovered that when you concentrated your efforts, when you really focused (with the help of your "Personal Checklist") on the task at hand, you succeeded in getting what you wanted—the time.

Always remember, no matter how trivial the situation, you must learn that it matters. Your ultimate success in this world—your ultimate success in getting what you really want out of life—depends on your day-to-day successes.

We've become so sophisticated, so out of touch with basics, we can only see the pot of gold that waits at the end of the rainbow. We forget about the treasures to be discovered along its path. If Dorothy had gone directly to Oz, she would have missed out on the Tin Man and the Cowardly Lion, not to mention all her adventures along the way.

Your strength will be developed by coming from a place of power—coming from live events. Building that pillar of strength makes the ultimate reward of achievement all the more gratifying.

THE BEVERLY HILLS STYLE

Treat every event in your life as a challenge, and it will soon become a game.

I'm often amused by the traveling companions most people choose: stacks of newspapers, magazines, every book they've been meaning to read for the last six months, letters they've been wanting to answer, and all their paperwork that's been left unattended. You'd think they'd rented a suite in an office instead of buying a ticket to paradise. A paradise that exists not at the end of their journey, but within their own heads—their land of dreams come true, their future reality.

I used to travel that way; you wouldn't see my blue eyes from takeoff to landing—they'd be fixated on the stack of work in front of me. Going on tour with my first book changed all that. In the two years I crisscrossed the United States and traveled around the world, I barely spent a moment alone and was always on the go. I had to react, respond, smile, and be on from 6 A.M. until 2 A.M. Believe me, I'm not complaining—I loved every second of it, but I soon discovered that three hours a night for sleep was simply not enough time to "let it all hang out," to recharge my batteries—to reflect and think things through. And, most important, to plan and dream. It was then that I discovered the wonders of vehicles of transportation—they stop the world, and give you time to get off.

The time you spend on them, be it five minutes, or five hours, is time out of time, time in between. You leave the world when you board, and you don't return to it until you get off. It's an isolated space in time, and you're a captive audience. A captive to your own dreams.

Always remember: all reality, even skyscrapers and bridges, begins with a dream. Before a bridge is built it's someone's idea. A skyscraper can't be erected until someone designs it. Your wish would be your command if you just took the time to think about it. Concentration is Go Power's gasoline. It's your ability to concentrate, to focus on your thoughts and what you want, that will fuel your Go Power and make it work for you. Use this "time out of time" to create your future; take advantage of it.

Scene 1. **STOP THE WORLD, I WANT TO GET OFF**
Objective: To Develop Your Powers of Concentration So That
    You Can Begin to Focus Energy

For the next week, whenever you find yourself on or in a bus, a train, a plane, or a car (passenger only, please), *surrender.* Put down your newspaper—close your attaché case—put away your book. Forget about your fellow commuters. Just lean back and close your eyes. Do what you did when you were in school and wanted to tune out the teacher: daydream. If you're a round-trip commuter, you only need to do it in one direction. However, try alternating between coming and going, and see how equally beneficial, yet different, they are.

If you don't commute or find yourself a passenger on anything, you'll have to put yourself on something. Take a bus ride to the end of the line, a taxi to nowhere, a train to the next town. It is important that you do this at least five times before moving on to the next scene.

If you're worried about when you'll find the time to do all those things that you used to do while commuting, let me remind you that there are 1,440 minutes in a day, so I'm sure you'll find it somewhere. Why not try reading your newspaper during the TV commercials? It's a lot less fattening than going to the refrigerator. Try going to the office a little earlier, stay a little later. Not only will you score points, you'll be a lot more productive if you finish your work at your desk instead of on a jiggling train.

What you will be doing is a form of meditation, of which there are many. Most are far more structured: TM (Transcendental Meditation), SMC (Silva Mind Control), not to be confused with SOM (Science of Mind), Hare Krishna, ad infinitum. Though all are infinitely different from one another—each having its own guru, chant, or mantra—their goals are similar: they teach relaxation techniques to reduce stress and to develop and utilize powers of concentration. VOTM (Vehicle of Transportation meditation)— my name for it—though beneficial as a relaxation technique, is not structured enough to *really* create any of the enormous changes you'd like to effect in your life. That power will come with a bit more discipline in your focus, a slightly more structured form of meditation.

In a structured form of meditation you practice it daily, *for* a specific time. A mantra (a sound or chant) is used to quiet the mind. While you are going to do something similar, your new discipline is going to remain very much an undiscipline.

Scene 2.   IT'S MAGIC
Objective: To Focus Your Energy to Create Miracles/or How to Succeed in Getting What You Want

In the meditation you are about to begin, you will not have a mantra. You see, the ancient Sanskrit word mantra actually means "wherever the mind wanders, explore it." Precisely what I want to happen. I don't really want to quiet your mind—I want it to wander, I want your thoughts and your imagination to run free. I want you to explore. Sooner or later, your mind will settle down, and when it does, it will automatically focus on the things you want most. If you focus on something negative, something that's troubling you or causing you anxiety, allow yourself to explore it, too. Your focus will help you effect a resolution. As the mind is free-flowing, new thoughts will enter and ultimately take precedence. The negative thoughts will leave of their own volition.

Your Beverly-Hills-Style *"Exploration"* must become a twenty-minute daily ritual. Although doing it at the same specific time every day is not necessary, until this new practice becomes as natural as brushing your teeth in the morning it's a good idea to do so. Often, until a discipline has been totally integrated into our lives, until it becomes something we want to do rather than something we have to do, we tend to forget to do it until it's too late. I don't want you to be in bed about to close your eyes and suddenly remember that you forgot to "explore." I don't want to hear, "Oh, well, I'll make up for it tomorrow." If you follow Scarlett O'Hara's philosophy and put off thinking about everything until tomorrow, you'll make getting everything you want one day further away. Haven't you wasted enough time? Haven't you been waiting long enough?

Could you survive being stranded alone on a desert island? If the stock-market crash of 1929 were to happen today, and you were an investor who lost everything, would you throw yourself out of a window? If your paycheck stopped and all visible means of support were to end and you had nowhere to go and no one to turn to—if there weren't unemployment and welfare didn't exist, if there were no food-stamp program—would you be able to feed and clothe yourself and pay the rent? What would you do if you had never worked a day in your life, had only a few close friends, and your entire family consisted of a husband, four small children, and a big dog with a big appetite, and one day your husband left for work and just never came home again?

Are you resourceful enough to take care of yourself, to be totally independent? You probably don't think so, but you are. And once you realize it, once you realize just what you can do, believe me you'll be able to do *anything*. Your wish will be your command, and *no star* will be too far away.

Scene 3.   HELP! MY SNOWMAN'S BURNING DOWN
Objective: To Develop the Resources Within Yourself to Face
Emergencies and Be Totally Independent

I want you to earn $25. I know it sounds easy enough. You probably make a lot more than that in a day. But there's a catch: you're not going to earn this money in your usual manner, or in a traditional way. Don't worry, you won't have to do anything illegal, immoral, or impossible—just creative.

You are going to create a way of earning at least $25 (which you will give to charity), based on your own natural resources—*your* creativity, *your* will, and *your* determination. You can't use money from your paycheck or sell your services in your usual occupation.

Since you may not have the vaguest idea of what you could possibly do, allow me to offer a few suggestions:

1. Make candy or bake cookies and sell them to your neighbors or co-workers.
2. Clean out your closets, attic, even the garage, and have a garage sale.
3. Sell raffle tickets for a nominal price and raffle yourself—well, your services for a day—maid, cook, shopper, or chauffeur (you'd be wise to limit your sale to people you know).
4. Mow lawns.
5. Wash cars.
6. Babysit.
7. Organize an adult spoof olympics with zany games (gunny-sack and one-legged race, egg roll and pass-the-grapefruit-neck-to-neck); charge an entry fee to participants and entrance fee to spectators.
8. Sell some of your new *(ahem)* creative works.
9. Throw a Monday night football party or a theater party for your friends in front of your television. Charge a small admission fee and make a load of popcorn and sell it. If you tell your friends what you're doing, I'm sure they won't balk at having to pay to sit on your floor.
10. Invite your friends over for a quasi casino night or play house games—Monopoly, backgammon, Trivial Pursuit—for money.
11. Ask a local merchant to donate services or a product and sell raffle tickets. Beauty salons could contribute a shampoo and set, manicures and pedicures; restaurants a dinner or lunch for two. Approach a hardware store, try for a toaster or an iron, but if all they'll give you is a set of Tupperware, take it.
12. If you knit or sew, make a sweater, baby clothes, something beautiful you can sell for $25.

I'm sure that now that I've sparked your fire, you'll think of many other lucrative and perhaps much more amusing money-making ideas. When you tap into your strengths, I'm sure you'll find many hidden resources—the most important one being you.

P.S. Don't forget, you are not allowed to keep any of the money you earn. Even if you earn more than the required $25, it must all be given to the charity of your choice.

Believe me, your good deed will not go unnoticed. Easterners call it Karma. Westerners call it the laws of retribution. Your energy is a magnet, it draws back to you whatever you put out.

Give and so shall you get. Including the best of everything!

When you've completed this scene, please fill in the following certificate and mail it or a copy of it to me at 270 North Cañon Drive, Beverly Hills, California 90212. What fun it will be to tally the total charitable donations from readers! I'll let you know the results.

CHARITY CERTIFICATE

NAME: _____

ADDRESS: _____

CITY/STATE: _____

MEANS OF RAISING MONEY: _____

AMOUNT RAISED: _____ AMOUNT DONATED: _____

You may reimburse yourself from the proceeds for your expenses, if you had any—legitimate expenses only, please (not to exceed $5).

CHARITY DONATED TO: _____

DATE OF DONATION: _____

Scene 4. **BODY AND SOUL**
Objective: To Achieve Physical "Perfection" and Develop Powers of Concentration and Focus Through Body Control

The world has gone exercise-crazy. Kenny Rogers can't live without tennis, Jacqueline Bisset without swimming, Bruce Dern without jogging, Jane Fonda without aerobics, and Jill St. John without yoga. Cathy Lee Crosby works out on a trapeze for two hours to battle the blues, Lynda Carter plays tennis, Kristy Mc-Nichol goes to dance class; even James Stewart is an exercise devotée.

Experts tell us that exercise is a major factor in helping us cope with problems, by reducing stress and tension, as well as controlling appetite.

And indeed, if all exercise does for us is allow us to vent hostility and repressed anger, that's certainly nothing to sneer at. I certainly didn't go to psychiatrists and augment my physical exercise routine (I've done it all, from jogging, a marathon included, to pelota) with the many different forms of the psychological modality called Body Therapy (Reichian therapy, Bioenergetics, Rolfing, the Alexander technique, Dance Therapy, Vocal Biomatrix) and not see an improvement in my mental attitude.

But the real change in me occurred when, like the Olympic divers and gymnasts, I changed from mindless exercise to a routine that required concentration and focus. I really began taking control when I began taking control of my body—when I became aware of my body, when I knew how it worked. When I thought about making it work, it really began to take shape. Just like magic, the lumps and bumps and little wads of nothing (atrophied muscles, all those muscles I hadn't used in years that had turned to jelly, a fringe benefit of our modern conveniences) disappeared. My once short-fat then short-skinny legs became longer—yes, one inch longer—and very shapely. The hunch in my shoulders, an area of lifelong concern, disappeared. I didn't have to stand on my tiptoes and stretch out of my body to reach 5′ 4″; my spine straightened, and I seemed to have grown taller. And all this had happened in barely six weeks. It was a miracle!

One of my miracle workers was the Lotte Berke Method. Developed by Lotte Berke in London, it was brought to this country and adapted by Lydia Bach fifteen years ago. The method combines an original technique with ballet, modern dance, hatha-yoga, and orthopedic exercises in a system of concentrated movements. You really have to think about what you're doing to do it, and it's not easy, but the results—well, they can speak for themselves: Ursula

Andress, Maude Adams, Candice Bergen, Pia Zadora, Shirley (Mrs. Henry) Fonda, Margaux Hemingway, Ali McGraw—all are proponents of the method. (Men, you're in luck—a new program has been developed especially for you, and classes have recently begun.)

There are Lotte Berke Method studios in Los Angeles and New York. See page 263 for information about Lydia's book and my tape.

But Lotte Berke is only half of it. I know I've mentioned that I've spent a lot of time with a number of celebrities, but did I tell you I've been swinging with them too? Literally, that is. Tony Bennett, Carrie Fisher, Barbara Walters, Michael Bennett, Susan Anton, Bulgari, Bill Murray—we've all discovered that there is more to exercise than meets the muscle.

"Stretch up, and you'll feel up," Jan Piatezk says, smiling, and you can't help but feel "up," plus a little like Olga Korbut, when you have your own Russian coach, as you reach to infinity and you realize that there is no limit to your potential. When you stretch your body, you stretch yourself. When you put your head into it, you can do anything.

My other miracle workers? Gymnastics and Alex and Walter, with studios in Los Angeles and New York. Gymnastics really connects your brain with your muscles. Can you imagine yourself doing tricks on the rings, or a trapeze? It's the next best thing to running away with the circus, but it's not just all fun and games; it also reunites your "Body and Soul."

Aside from the actual physical improvement and improved concentration techniques, gymnastics has also enabled me to change my mental attitude. I've learned a lot about trust and risk-taking, not only how they apply to what goes on in the studio, but in all the other aspects of my life as well. Diving head first onto the floor in front of you and knowing—well, hoping—you won't break your neck (a dive roll) is really taking a risk. Leaning backward on a trapeze, or balancing on it, on your hipbones—"look ma, no hands" and trusting the someone that's there spotting you to catch you, is having a lot of trust. It all carries over.

You don't have to wait until you are in Beverly Hills or New

York to go to Alex and Walter's although if you're there you must. There are gymnastic classes almost everywhere, so check the yellow pages in your telephone directory.

Insisting that you do a specific exercise is something I'll never do, no matter how strongly I believe in it for myself. The Lotte Berke Method and gymnastics—my miracle workers—although not crucial to your ultimate success, will only make it a lot easier and a lot quicker. I do encourage, in fact I insist, that you do something physical every day, even if it's only a walk around the block. But most important, whatever you do must be of your own choosing and it should be fun for you.

When was the last time you gave yourself a pat on the back or felt pride in having accomplished something? Probably when you did, yours wasn't the only pat you got. It's easy to reap praise for your major achievements, for your great performances, but what about your little triumphs, the ones that no one else notices, the ones that you barely even notice? Don't they deserve something?

Have you ever made a shopping list for yourself, or mapped out your daily activities, ticking them off one by one as they were accomplished? Isn't that achieving a goal? Didn't that achievement require some will and determination on your part? Now, I'm certainly not suggesting that calling the dentist and making an appointment means you're a great success, but at least you accomplished what you set out to do. Remember, your success in this world and your success in getting what you really want will ultimately depend upon your day-to-day successes. It's the totality of your day-to-day successes that are turning *you* into one.

ACT II   PROPS: Pencil
                              Notebook

Scene 1. THE PROUD AND THE BEAUTIFUL
Objective: To Experience a Sense of Pride in Your Day-to-Day
    Successes

Beginning tonight, and every night for at least the next three
weeks, write all your accomplishments of the day in your workbook (minimum: three per day). Preface each accomplishment
with, "I'm so proud of myself, I . . ." (then add what you did).
Remember, this does not mean major achievements. It means all
the things you do that you take for granted, that you should instead
take pride in: you got to work on time, you did the breakfast dishes,
you made your bed, you didn't oversleep, you cleared out a closet.
Take your workbook to bed with you and do your list right before
you close your eyes. Go to sleep on the most positive note.

To ensure that you'll also wake up on a positive note and begin
each day with a smile, read this list aloud as soon as you open your
eyes in the morning. Don't worry if you're not alone—your bed
partner shouldn't mind. If he/she didn't think you were pretty
terrific, he/she wouldn't be there. Besides, it will serve as a good
reminder if one is needed.

Scene 2. YESTERDAY, TODAY, AND TOMORROW
Objective: To Focus On, Go After, and Begin Realizing Goals

We're all motivated by our goals. It's our need to achieve that
encourages us to forge ahead. Unfortunately, the tendency is to see
only our long-range goals, and all too often we give up on them
because of our "unrealistic" expectation that they should have been
realized yesterday. If becoming a millionaire is one of your goals,
then attaining that is all you can see, and you're apt to discount
everything that comes before it. The nickels and dimes don't

count—nothing else "counts," only the ultimate achievement of the ultimate goal. Unfortunately, if you don't go on the journey, you'll never reach your destination!

Following you'll find your Yesterday, Today, and Tomorrow goal sheet. Your list should include only your immediate goals, the sort of goals that could realistically become reality in six to eight weeks. Since we often tend not to think of our daily activities as goals, I've given you a hand by making a list of some of the goals that one could expect to achieve in that period of time. If some of them seem silly to you, remember not everyone wants the same things. Thank goodness for that. Just think of how tough the competition would be if they did. If I've listed any of *your* goals, make them your own by checking them off. My list is meant to be a helpmate and certainly not *your* final word. I'm sure I haven't thought of everything you want, so I've left plenty of space for your additions.

Please note: at the close of this chapter, you'll find your Showdown Syllabus with Fulfillment Aids. They are listed according to the numbers in parentheses.

A word of caution before you begin: Don't overshoot your mark! If you do, if you aren't realistic, *nothing* will get accomplished. Your frustration will see to that. If things don't happen as quickly as you'd like, just keep telling yourself that what you didn't get yesterday and what you can't have today will be yours tomorrow. Just be patient, and before you know it, a tree will grow in Brooklyn.

YESTERDAY, TODAY, AND TOMORROW GOALS

I'll get to work on time (1)
I'll get up on time (1)
I'll clean up the breakfast dishes before I leave the house (1)
I'll have time to make my bed in the morning (1)
I won't be late for any of my appointments (1)
I'll stop smoking (2)
I'll stick to my diet (3)
I'll stop yelling at the children (4)

I won't fight with my husband (4)
I'll ask for a raise (5)
I'll ask for a promotion (5)
I'll look for a new job (6)
I'll get a new job (7)
I'll start exercising (8)
I'll clean the attic/garage/closets (9)
I'll keep my car clean (9)
I'll write letters/answer correspondence (10)
I'll balance my checkbook as soon as I receive my bank statement (11)
I'll take my clothes to the cleaners/do the laundry before they/it piles up (9)
I'll be more organized (12)
I'll return telephone calls (13)
I'll stop drinking (14)
I'll smile more often (15)
I'll stop talking on the phone incessantly (16)
I'll spend more time with my children/husband/wife (17)
I'll go to bed earlier (18)
I'll read more (19)
I'll go to church/temple (20)

If you can't think of at least five goals, you aren't thinking about YOU.

1. I'll _____
2. I'll _____
3. I'll _____
4. I'll _____
5. I'll _____

Scene 3. A TREE GROWS IN BROOKLYN
Objective: To Focus On, Go After, and Begin Realizing Goals of Greater Magnitude—Goals That Could Take as Long as a Year.

I hope there are many goals in your life that, while not as simplistic as getting your car washed, are still somewhat easier to attain than becoming a millionaire. Isn't being nominated best actress almost as important as actually taking Oscar home?

Always remember, the fulfillment of one goal will lead to the next.

Robert Mitchum might have had stardom in mind when he set his sights on Hollywood, but I'm sure he was still mighty happy when he got that first walk-on. At least it was a chance to be seen!

Can I Do It Till I Need Glasses was a far cry from *Popeye,* but at least Robin Williams was on the silver screen. It was a chance to practice his on-camera technique!

Making millions laugh on national television is a bit grander than making a handful laugh at The Comedy Store in Westwood, California, but without The Comedy Store as a stepping-stone, *The David Letterman Show* might not have become a reality. It was a chance to develop that amazing timing!

Once again, I've listed a few examples as guidelines to the type of goals you can expect to realize within a year. Obviously these should be goals that you've already given some thought to and have already started working on. Once again, if any of mine are yours, you may have them. No Fulfillment Aids now, you've moved onto the big screen—you're on your own.

A TREE GROWS IN BROOKLYN GOALS

Get a new job	**Get a fur coat**
Get thin	**Get married**
Buy a car	**Get divorced**
Move	**Start a new business**
Take the QE2 to London	**Panel the basement**

Scene 4. **THE SKY'S THE LIMIT**
Objective: Realizing Your Heart's Desires

You'll see that the goal page is blank. I've given you no clues, no hints, and no guidelines because the Sky's the Limit. This page is all yours—your hopes, your dreams, your heart's desire. There are no time limits. When they happen doesn't matter. This is an ongoing page that you should be adding to for the rest of your life.

THE SKY'S THE LIMIT GOALS

SHOWDOWN SYLLABUS

Obviously, your goal is to *achieve* your goal. Believe me, if your GO POWER is really on, and if you're really using your DFC (Dedication, Focus, and Concentration—remember?), your dreams will soon become your reality.

You don't need me to tell you that if something is worthwhile, it's not going to come easy. If it did, you'd already have it. Since it's easy to get lazy when the going gets tough or things don't happen right away, you'll need to keep a close surveillance on yourself; a re-evaluation, as it were, on a regular basis.

Your Re-evaluation Timetable along with an example of a Showdown Synopsis Sheet follows.

If you send me copies of your Showdown Synopsis Sheets when your goals are realized, I'll send you a GO FOR GOAL award for each one. With the first award, you'll also receive information and an application for the Showdown Shootout. Sorry, you'll have to do something first to find out what it's all about.

Send your sheets to:

THE BEVERLY HILLS STYLE
GO FOR GOAL AWARD
270 North Cañon Drive
Beverly Hills, California 90212

RE-EVALUATION TIMETABLE

YESTERDAY, TODAY AND TOMORROW GOALS—Every
2nd Thursday
A TREE GROWS IN BROOKLYN GOALS—The 7th Day of the
Month
THE SKY'S THE LIMIT GOALS—The 11th Day of Alternate
Months

GO-FOR-GOAL RANKINGS

DEDICATION TO EXCELLENCE
1. Sloppy
2. Slightly amiss
3. Not bad
4. Getting a lot better
5. Hot

FOCUS
1. Out of Control
2. Cross-eyed
3. It's in My Mind's Eye
4. I've Got It Covered
5. On a Clear Day I Can See Forever

CONCENTRATION
1. I must have amnesia, my mind's a total blank
2. Out of sight, out of mind
3. Stick it to me
4. The watched pot is boiling
5. Bullseye

SHOWDOWN SYNOPSIS SHEET

DATE	GO ON (Check)	DEDICATION TO EXCELLENCE Rank (1-5)	FOCUS Rank (1-5)	CONCENTRATION Rank (1-5)

FULFILLMENT AIDS

Fulfillment Aids are simple techniques that have proven successful in helping people fulfill specific goals. If some seem a bit simplistic, unrealistically easy, it's only because before you read this book you were making too big a deal out of everything—making it all much more difficult than it actually is. If you have tried before and failed, you must not let past failure defeat you. It's different now; not only are you ready for success, your Go Power is on and your DFC is operating. You can't miss! Believe me, it's all as easy as it sounds.

Note: Each Fulfillment Aid is numbered to correspond to the number in parentheses that follow the goals listed on the "Yesterday, Today, and Tomorrow" goal sheet.

(1)
I'll get to work on time.
I'll get up on time.
I'll clean up the breakfast dishes.
I'll make my bed in the morning.
I won't be late for any of my appointments.

Time, my friend, has a way of running out. If you keep running late, you're going to keep coming in last. It's boring always to be harried and hassled and apologizing.

Step 1.
You must always be aware of time. Wear a wristwatch at all times. Surround yourself with snooze-alarm clocks, clocks that have special buttons that, when depressed, will re-ring the alarm five minutes later. You are to have three clocks within your sight at all times. If you are in a fairly permanent location—a desk in an office, for instance—keep the three clocks on your desk; one on your left, one on your right, and one directly in front of you.

Step 2.
Each night before you go to sleep, on a 3x5 card fill out a daily Time Allowance for the following day, listing your permanent as well as your "tomorrow only" commitments in sequential order at the specific times they must be done.

Not all your permanent time commitments are a problem. There are some things you just do automatically. If you have included any of those on this list, cross them out.

Include on your card the time of the commitment (your "when"), how long it will take to get there (your "how long"), how much time you'll need to do it, and the SA (signal alert).

The SA, which is *always* fifteen minutes ahead of the time that you must leave for the commitment, is the time that all three alarm clocks will be set for every commitment: For example, if my commitment or arrival time is 1:00 P.M. and it will take me twenty minutes to get there, I would set the alarm for 12:25. When the first alarm goes off, it is a fifteen-minute warning; prepare accordingly. You are permitted to hit the snooze button twice. The third time it rings you are to turn off the alarm from the main switch, stop whatever else you were doing, check your Time Allowance card for your next commitment, set the alarms accordingly, and get the hell out and go do whatever it is you are supposed to be doing.

(2)
I'll stop smoking

Day 1.
Three days prior to stopping you will do two things.

Step 1.
Sit alone in a comfortable chair in a quiet room and close your eyes and relax. Imagine yourself giving in to an impulse that is almost too ridiculous to imagine. For example, walking down the street naked or robbing a bank or punching your boss in the mouth, even hanging up on your mother-in-law or throwing a cream pie at your husband. Really give it some thought; don't just use my examples. This is *your* situation, only you know what's too ridiculous for you. Allow the image to linger in your mind's eye; visualize it clearly, in color if you can. Focus on it, concentrate on it. Keep the image alive for five minutes. For the next two hours recapture it whenever you can—allow it to linger for a minute or two.

Step 2.
Enlist a close friend or relative to become your Smoke Signal. This should be someone to whom you have twenty-four-hour-a-day access, a nonsmoker. Tell your friend that you are going to stop smoking on (appropriate day, three days hence) and that you will be calling whenever you want a cigarette. Remember, that call is important. You must make it. Under no circumstances are you to try to get through this without calling. Your Smoke Signal is to give you one response, and one response only, recited verbatim:

"How ridiculous, why would you want a cigarette when you don't smoke? Do you give in to all your other impulses, too? How ridiculous!" [This exact phraseology is important. Don't trust it to memory. It should be written down and kept next to every telephone in his or her house.]

Day 2.

Step 1.

Alert your Smoke Signal that tomorrow is D-Day. Verify that the phrase is next to each telephone. Check personally, if necessary.

Step 2.

Before you go to bed fill out a 3x5 card with the following message: THANK GOD I DON'T SMOKE CIGARETTES. Place the card against the back of your alarm clock. It should be hitting the turn-off knob.

Step 3.

Fill out a 3x5 card with the message "You're right, how ridiculous, I don't give in to my other impulses, why would I give in to a cigarette, especially since I don't smoke cigarettes? Thank God, I don't smoke cigarettes." A card with this message is to be propped up on every telephone in your house. You should have one extra card that is with you and accessible at all times.

Step 4.

Allow the ridiculous mental image you conjured up earlier to reappear in your mind's eye, and concentrate on it for five minutes. Then immediately turn out the lights, close your eyes, let your image flash once more, and go to sleep.

Day 3.

As you reach to shut off your alarm, grasp the 3x5 card in your hand and immediately repeat the sentence, "Thank God I don't smoke cigarettes," aloud. You must call your Smoke Signal as often as the urge to smoke strikes—every time you even so much as think about a cigarette, pick up that phone. Don't worry about calling too often. Your Smoke Signal wants to help you and is glad you asked. If a phone isn't available to you or your Smoke Signal is not home, just hold on, keep trying to reach her, and don't take so much as a puff. Keep reminding yourself that the cigarette will still be there later if you still want it—it's not going anywhere, and you can wait.

A typical phone call should go like this:

YOU: I have to have a cigarette, I'll die if I don't have one, I'm going crazy.

THEY: How ridiculous, why would you want a cigarette when you don't smoke? Do you give in to all your impulses? How ridiculous!

YOU (Allowing your ridiculous image to flash in your mind's eye and see it clearly): "You're right, how ridiculous, I don't give in to all my other impulses, why should I give in to a cigarette? Especially since I don't smoke. Thank God I don't smoke cigarettes." [Wouldn't you feel like a real jerk if you lit a cigarette now?]

Gradually your desire to smoke will diminish, along with your dependency on your Smoke Signal—I hope before he or she gets a new telephone number. Don't expect it to happen in a second; this could take weeks, maybe even months. "Thank God I don't smoke cigarettes" will become an automatic internal response to any remaining desire to smoke and will eventually and automatically squelch that urge. It's gradual, it's natural, and it's unconscious; it just happens. You'll feel it when it does. THANK GOD YOU DON'T SMOKE CIGARETTES!

(3)
I'll stick to my diet

I don't care if you've been on a million diets, done a million programs, gone to a million experts, and gained and lost more than you weigh now a million times. You've never really been ready to be thin before. Your Go Power has never been on before and you've never known how to use your DFC to help you. You only have to be successful once, and this could be it, so you might as well try. Well, what have you got to lose?

The word "diet" is actually a Latin word meaning "a way of

life," or "food habitually consumed." However, when the word is used to describe a weight-loss regimen, it refers to a disciplined eating program geared toward weight reduction. Any weight-loss program will work if you stick to it.

Day 1.

Step 1.

Find a diet that you feel confident you'll be able to stick to. Most bookstores have entire sections devoted to diet, so plan to spend some time looking through them all to find yours. Don't necessarily pick the one that everybody is doing or that's on the bestseller list. Just because it's popular doesn't necessarily mean it will work for you. If it doesn't include either foods and/or a lifestyle that's consistent with yours, it will do the same thing its predecessors have done—stop working. And once again you'll feel like a big fat failure. Only *you* can make it work, and now you *can.*

Step 2.

Once you've found your diet, read Fulfillment Aid #2. Do Step 1.

Step 3.

Select and delegate a Skinny Voice—the dieter's version of the smoker's Smoke Signal.

Step 4.

Announce your intentions *to get thin* (not lose weight) three days before you are going to begin your diet. Give your Skinny Voice his or her phrase as well as enough written copies on 3x5 cards for all the telephones in the house: "How ridiculous, I thought you were getting thinner every day. Do you give in to all your impulses? If you eat now, you won't get thinner. Why do you want to get fat again?" Visualize *your* ridiculous mental image, and repeat the recall process as described in Fulfillment Aid #2 for two days.

Day 2.

Step 1.

Do Day 2, Step 1 of Fulfillment Aid #2.

Step 2.

Before going to sleep place a 3x5 card in back of your alarm clock with *your* response, "I'm getting thinner every day. Thank God I'm not fat any more and I'll never be fat again." (You must use the word "fat," even if you're not exactly what one would describe as fat.)

Step 3.

Fill out a second 3x5 card with your response for all your telephones and carry one with you at all times. Visualize your mental image. Turn out the lights, let that image flash again and go to sleep.

Day 3.

Step 1.

Recite *your* phrase aloud the moment you've turned off your alarm. Call your Skinny Voice WHENEVER YOU NEED TO: whenever you have the urge to eat when you shouldn't, or eat something you shouldn't. Do not try to get through even one moment of madness behind the fat curtain alone. If you could have done it alone, you would have been thin long before now. Don't worry about calling too often. Your Skinny Voice has willingly become your support system; his or her skinny little shoulders are stronger than you think. Remember, only you can pick up that phone, only you can make the call. Only *you* can make this work. If you want to get thin you'll do it; if you don't, it's only because Thin isn't really a goal of yours and shouldn't be on your goal list.

A typical call should go like this:

YOU: I want to eat, if I don't eat something, I'll die, I have to have some Haagen Daz chocolate chocolate chip right now. I'm going cra-a-a-zy!

SKINNY VOICE: How ridiculous! I thought you were getting thinner every day. Do you give in to all your impulses? If you eat now, you won't get thinner. Why do you want to get fat again?

YOU: You're right, how ridiculous! [Close your eyes and see your ridiculous image in all its fat, glorious color.] I am

getting thinner every day. Thank God I'm not fat anymore, and I'll never be fat again.

Close your eyes again, recall your image, and grab a wad of fat. If
you can't find a wad of fat, you shouldn't be trying to lose weight.
The anorexic look may be fashionable, but it's certainly not very
attractive.

A word of caution: Don't choose a fat person to be your Skinny
Voice; his or her own guilt feelings, intensified by your strength,
will ultimately undermine you.

(4)
I'll stop yelling at the children
I won't fight with my husband/wife

As Archie Bunker would say, "Stifle yourself." When the urge to
yell strikes, clench your lips and your fists, drop back three yards
and punt. Then count to ten. Keep going back to one, until
whatever created your urge to yell has stopped. Nothing can continue indefinitely, including "those little brats" or that "you know
what."

Remember, for every action there is a reaction. Many actions are
done strictly for our benefit, to elicit our reaction, and if we don't
react, the action is in vain and ceases to have a purpose. Sooooo, get
smart and "vain" them out! In fact, why don't you initiate an
action to elicit *their* reaction? How do you think most people
would react to love and affection?

(5)
I'll ask for a raise
I'll ask for a promotion

Ask for it.

(6)
I'll look for a new job

Look for it.

(7)
I'll get a new job

Get it.

Note: If 5, 6, and 7 are not possible, if it is still "not quite that simple," then you aren't ready yet so just move these goals to "A Tree Grows in Brooklyn." Once you get a little stronger, a little more confident, you'll be able to reach them.

(8)
I'll start exercising

An exercise program must be started slowly if you want to integrate it into your routine successfully. If you try to do too much, it becomes too much, and, before you know it, it's another one of those "I tried it and. . . ." Until you get into the swing of it, do something that won't take a lot of time—let your frustration come from not doing enough and wanting more, rather than doing too much and wanting out.

Don't run right out and join a health club. You'll just be wasting your money, you won't go. If you want to go to an organized class, fine, just don't sign up for any series: it's pay as you go *only*.

Maximum two classes a week, in the beginning. If you start out with an unrealistic routine, often the case with the born-again exerciser, your guilt feelings at not being able to keep it up will cause you to give it up. If after one month you want to increase the classes, then by all means do so. Exercise must always be something you really want to do; you'll never do it, if you feel as if you have to do it.

Your best bet to begin would be to do something you can do on your own, something that's easy, convenient, and free. Then you'll never be able to say you can't afford it. If it's something close to home, travel and time can never be used as an excuse. Walking is great, and it doesn't require any athletic prowess. Well, at least not in the beginning, not until you've *really* begun to clip along. Don't start out with two miles—that's ridiculous, you'll never do it. No, you won't even keep up one mile either. When I say start slow, I mean *start slow*. For the first three days try one block each way. Then every three days increase it by half a block each way, until you reach a distance that you're comfortable with. Maintain that distance until you're forced to go farther; when the distance you're doing is simply not enough, you *must* do more. An exercise program should always leave you a little hungry—if you're underfed, you'll want more and you'll continue doing it.

(9)
I'll clean the attic/garage/closets
I'll keep my car clean
I'll take my clothes to the cleaners before they pile up

In bold letters, label giant green garbage bags with whatever needs to be cleaned up. For instance, closet trash, garage trash, car trash. Pile them in front of their appropriate area, right where you can see them. In front of the closet. In front of the garage (the inside house entrance). On the front seat of your car. There's only one escape from the Jolly Green Eyesore: the bags will be full and out of the way real soon.

(10)
I'll write letters/answer correspondence

Keep stationery and unanswered correspondence on your nightstand and work on it at night, before you go to sleep. In the morning take any leftover correspondence and put it in the middle of your bed after you've made it. You'll get very bored moving that pile back and forth.

(11)
I'll balance my checkbook as soon as I receive my bank statement

Open your bank statement as soon as you get it. Sort and lay checks out on your bed numerically. If you don't finish them, stack them on your nightstand in a pile before you go to sleep. In the morning, again lay them out numerically on your bed, after you've made it. *Boring.*

(12)
I'll be more organized

Keep a stack of 3x5 cards on your nightstand. Begin tonight to organize tomorrow. Get a head start on the day. List everything you need to do. Carry the card with you at all times and add to it accordingly. Tick off items when completed. Take your card to bed with you. Any uncompleted items should head your list for the next day. Penalize yourself for each uncompleted task or item: one dollar for each in a little bank to be opened and spent only when you've gotten through a day with no carryovers.

(13)
I'll return telephone calls

Set aside a designated time every day in which returning calls takes precedence over anything else, and adhere to it. Simply do not let *anything* interfere.

(14)
I'll stop drinking

Read Fulfillment Aids Number 2 and Number 3 thoroughly! Substitute a Thirst Quencher for Smoke Signal or Skinny Voice. Use the exact dialogues that the smoker uses (Fulfillment Aid Number 2), but substitute the word "drink" for "smoke," and "alcohol" for "cigarettes."

(15)
I'll smile more

What have you got to be unhappy about? Well, whatever it is, resolving it should be your goal. Starting off the day on a positive note will help to put a smile on your face. Use your "I'm So Proud of Myself" List, page 85. If you think back to some of the scenes you've been rehearsing, that will certainly be good for a laugh or two, and if all else fails—force it. Just pull back those lips and smile, and before you know it, you might even begin to believe it yourself.

(16)
I'll stop talking on the phone incessantly

Step 1.

Just as you are about to make your first telephone call of the day, grab one of your handy 3x5 cards. Write down three things you've thought about doing someday that could be done in the course of a day but you've never found the time to do before. (These should be three things that *do not* appear on any of your goal lists.)

Step 2.

Write down all the calls you *must* make that day. Remember, you're the one who wants to stop all this inane chatting, so be serious about it. Really consider what are, and what are not, "must" calls.

Step 3.

Every time you find yourself picking up the telphone, check your list. If you are not about to make a "must call," replace the receiver immediately and go to work on one of the three someday items heading your list. Check off your "must calls" as you make them. Once all your "must calls" are made, and you have done your three "somedays," the telephone's all yours, so chat away.

Once you've found other things to do that involve and reward you, the telephone will cease to be an outlet.

(17)
I'll spend more time with my children/husband/wife

As a family team, organize one specific time slot on a specific day when you will all—come hell or high water, business meetings or hockey practice—be together. There cannot be any excuses, it's as simple as that. Obviously, don't pick a time in which other things often come up. If you find that despite all your good intentions, you're canceling more family reunions than you're keeping, or certain specific members have a lot of great excuses for being late or not being there at all, try changing the time or the day. If that doesn't work, move this goal to "A Tree Grows in Brooklyn," and keep trying—eventually it will become a reality.

(18)
I'll go to bed earlier

With so many things piling up, on, and next to your bed, it seems like the logical place to be.

(19)
I'll read more

Having discovered so many new things in you, and in your world, I should think you'd want to read more. Go back to chapter two, Act 4, Scene 1, and re-rehearse that scene as it applies to you today.

(20)
I'll go to church/temple

Make a vow.

Close Encounters
of the First Kind

ALL THAT YOU ARE IS WHAT YOU THINK YOU ARE
I've always been very conscious of my body. I'm conscious of the
fact that it doesn't look like Burt Reynolds's. And he's probably
conscious of the fact that his doesn't look like mine . . .
—George Burns

**ALL THE WORLD WILL EVER SEE
IS WHAT YOU SHOW THEM**
Beauty without self-confidence is less attractive than ugliness with
self-confidence. If you are confident, you are beautiful.
—George Cukor

Any woman, even if she is supposed to be a beauty, can see defects
when she looks at herself in the mirror. But I have a very clear
picture of myself. It's not just a question of good features. . . . It's
what's inside you.
—Catherine Deneuve

ACT I   **PROPS:** Mirror
Telephone book
Telephone
Pencil
Money

Talk, talk, talk. What good is all this talk doing, you ask. It hasn't changed the fact that your ears still stick out like Dumbo's. The hairdresser you went to tried the Britt Eklund Hideaway, but you're not Britt Eklund, so the hair over the ear routine didn't quite make it. OK, OK, you did what I said, you not only bought *The Way Bandy Makeup Book*, but also another one that looked interesting. When you had tried all the tricks and they didn't work, you even went to a professional makeup artist. He broadened your cheekbones, widened your eyes, but you still look like Pinocchio. Maybe Sophia Loren could handle it, maybe she could ignore the comments that she should "trim a bit off her nose," but you can't. You know that one of the three standards others judge you by when you first meet them is the way you look, and the way you look doesn't make you very happy.

Even though you keep rereading your Physical Like list and checking your rankings on the chart in chapter two, and it has given you strength as has the list of famous people with physical disadvantages, it's not enough—*they* don't have to live with you. *They* don't have to look at you in the mirror.

Sure, sure, you know, you've heard it a million times. "Beauty is in the eye of the beholder." But who wants to "behold" a face that would stop a clock? And you keep reminding yourself, over and over again, that "beauty's only skin deep." But who, particularly someone you've just met, is going to dig?

"She is the actress-writer-photographer who symbolizes the great American dream of beauty—tall and slender with blonde streaked hair, tawny skin, fine-boned features, a dazzling smile and a husky melodic voice. . ."

Candice Bergen was lucky, she was born beautiful. Phyllis Diller wasn't quite that lucky. But look at her today. Believe me, if she can do it, if she can *become* beautiful, so can you!

Yes, Virginia, there is a Santa Claus, and he'll bring you a new nose, or put your ears on where they belong. He'll even wipe away those acne scars left from your youth. And if you pack up that extra chin in those satchels under your eyes, he'll take them away in his own. In fact, if you're a real good girl, he'll even let you give him your belly. He'll hardly even notice it, it's so easy for him to take away.

And maybe, just maybe, you'll get real lucky, like a famous television series actress whose Santa Claus was young and handsome, and who also turned out to be her knight in shining armor.

Thanks to people like Betty Ford, Phyllis Diller, and a handful of doctors, the myth has been shed; cosmetic surgery has come out of the closet. It's no longer just for the rich and famous, the movie stars and jet setters; in fact, if you were to walk into many a plastic surgeon's office you'd see very few aging society matrons amidst the throng of young professionals. Their average age is about forty.

I asked one prominent doctor what his patients were most concerned about. His eyes twinkling, he told me about the three-hundred-pound woman who came in dragging half of her behind her.

"A buttocks reduction?" I inquired.

"No." He laughed. "She wanted the excess skin removed from her elbows."

People aren't only concerned with their faces giving away their age as was the case of the flight attendant who looked as if she had had too many layovers in Miami. It wasn't the deeply embedded lines in her leatherlike skin that worried her; she wanted something done about the wrinkles on her knuckles.

The number of men seeking cosmetic surgery has more than doubled in the past fifteen years comprising about 30 percent of this doctor's clientele. Men are most concerned about their jobs and competition from the youth market. New noses and face lifts to give a younger look are what most of them are after, but quite a few have been asking for buttocks augmentation. (Sorry, it can't be done.)

You know when you think about it, a lot of those old-time actors must have had face lifts. I don't care how many fountain-of-youth treatments You Know Who claims to have gotten; he sure looks awfully good for his eighty-plus years. And for someone who'd been around as long as John Wayne, he sure looked good. And so did that other cowboy, Gary Cooper.

According to the doctors I interviewed, the biggest fear people have is getting a stretched-too-tight, masklike appearance "that

Norma Desmond look." (If you don't know who Norma Desmond is, then you're too young for a face lift.) As I said earlier, age is really no longer a guidepost. As a matter of fact, I happen to know that the Oscar-nominated English actress seen leaving a plastic surgeon's Madison Avenue office with her face swathed in bandages (most procedures are no longer done in the hospital) was born in 1941. How silly it is to wait until you *really* need it. Just think of all those trips to the mirror when you looked at yourself holding the skin stretched up from your jaw.

I asked this same doctor about a friend of mine, one of New York's "great faces," who looked at least thirty years younger than her reputed age. It has been said that this chanteuse-turned-author (her novel is a highly fictionalized account of her affair with a much younger international celebrity) cannot close her eyes; that her face is now devoid of all planes, and must be painted on daily. Supposedly the result of too many lifts.

"It's probably not from surgery," the good doctor said. "More likely, it is the result of an associated nonmedical procedure—dermabrasion—using a very strong chemical. For this very reason it is not frequently used. That look just doesn't happen with surgery."

"Tell me about a great success," I said, "about someone whose life was dramatically changed."

"Sorry to sound so boring," he replied. "Plastic surgery doesn't change lives, it just makes happier people. But I guess that happier people usually do accomplish more because they're more productive." He broke into a grin, as he realized just how many lives he had changed.

Yes, Virginia, there is a Santa Claus, and you won't even have to wait until Christmas. All you'll have to do is find yourself one, and tell him what you want. Only don't try the children's section in your local department store. Instead, look in the yellow pages or call your local Cosmetic Surgery Association.

Oh, that's not what's bothering you. It's that you're not Katharine Hepburn, so *you* can't get away with wearing a scarf on your head all the time. You can't just take the attitude that "it's all behind you," as so many *men* are inclined to do.

Well, a scarf or a wig is not your only alternative. You don't have to live with anything. Burt Reynolds had a choice, and he didn't go the Yul Brynner route, or learn to live with it. Baldness and thinning hair—it's no big deal, a dermatologist could help you with that: weaving, transplants—there's a world of choices.

If too *little* hair isn't exactly your problem, electrolysis may be your answer. It's quick as a prick and just as painless, according to international beauty expert Aida Grey, whose main salon is a tradition in Beverly Hills. "Electrolysis is like plucking an eyebrow."

Come on, let's have a little smile. What? What do you mean you don't smile? Oh, I see, now I understand why you won't smile. I wouldn't either if I had your teeth. Trust me, there's a solution for everyone and I have one for you that will have you grinning from ear to ear. But don't thank me, thank Beverly Hills dentist-to-the-superstars Stanley Vogel, who pioneered and perfected porcelain veneering, and New York dentist Irwin Smigel, president of the American Society for Dental Aesthetics, who revolutionized dentistry with his technique, called bonding. Not only will they or any of the scores of dentists using their techniques, have you smiling by the end of a day, there's almost no grinding or shots (in bonding there's none) and no pain. ESPECIALLY WHEN YOU HAVE TO PAY THE BILL. It's half the price of caps. In fact, almost anything you need done to yourself will probably only be the cost of a couple of vacations.

Phyllis Diller didn't have too much to smile about when she looked in the mirror more than fifteen years ago, but she sure has now. And soon, so will you.

Scene 1. **THE UGLY DUCKLING**
Objective: To Perfect the Physical You with Outside Help

Go to the mirror and look at yourself, front and back. Spend some time, *really* study yourself. Study your hair, your eyes, your nose—check them from all angles. Your ears, your lips. What about your skin; is it clear—is it very lined? How's that chin, or is it chins? Let's lift them up. Okay, let's have a great big smile. What about those teeth, are they straight and even—are they white? When was the last time you had them cleaned? Well, what do you think— is your age showing? Does that bother you—not your age, just that it's showing?

OK, now, get naked. That's right, naked, and stand in front of a full-length mirror. So what's the verdict? It's a lot better than it was, isn't it? Thighs, tummy, bosom, arms, buttocks. Is there any hope, will the sight of it *ever* turn you on? I know you're working on it, but do you think you'll ever be happy looking at yourself, no matter how much you exercise, no matter how many haircuts you get, despite all the makeup you use or the tricks you try?

Self-confidence? It's tough to have when you approach the world from a place of "if only." If only my cheeks didn't sag, if only that chipped tooth weren't so obnoxious, if only I hadn't eaten so much chocolate when I was a teen. "If only, if only, if only." It colors your world and changes your relationship to it. It becomes a part of your consciousness, an aspect of your attitude, your excuse to apologize.

Well, hold those chins up high, you have nothing that you need to apologize for. Everything that's wrong with you is fixable, so let's go get them fixed. There are enough obstacles in your life— you certainly don't need *you* against you too.

List all the physical flaws you still think you have, in the space below or in your workbook:

MY "IF ONLY," FIXABLE, PHYSICAL FLAWS

Go back over your Fixable Physical Flaw list. Be honest, have you really done, or are you doing, absolutely *everything* that you can do to improve each of them? If you're uncertain as to just how much you can do, reread chapter two, Act V Scene 2, reassessing and crossing out any flaws that could still be improved under your diligent tutelage.

I want you to hold off turning your thighs, buttocks, or belly over to a cosmetic surgeon for just a while longer. Give my Miracle Workers in "Body and Soul" (chapter four, Scene 4) three months to do what they can. Now take one more look at yourself and imagine how you're going to look after you've been all fixed up, after those "craftsmen" have done *their* jobs. Now it's time to find the appropriate ones and go see them.

Take a look at the following example of an Individual Consultation and Reappraisal chit. Fill one out for all remaining flaws on your list.

INDIVIDUAL CONSULTATION AND REAPPRAISAL CHIT
(sample)

FIXABLE, PHYSICAL FLAW	**(Area of improvement)**
FIXER	**(Type of specialist needed)**
MAGICIAN OF MENTION	**(Recommended specialist)**
ADDRESS	**TEL.:**
ON YOUR MARK	**(The date you called for an appointment)**
GET SET	**(The date of the appointment)**
GO (The consultation—a recap. Go through the session verbatim: what the doctor said, how you felt about him/her, how you felt about what he or she had to say, etc.)	
THE COST	**(Fill in amount)**
REAPPRAISAL	**(Explanation follows*)**

*Reappraisal:

The minute you return from the specialist, return to your mirror and re-examine the flaw in question. Rehash your consultation, asking yourself the following questions:

1. Is there anything else *I* can do before I turn myself over to this professional?
2. Does my flaw look any better to me now that I know I don't have to be stuck with it forever?
3. Is there any reason why I shouldn't take that positive step forward and do something about it now? Any good reason at all why I shouldn't get it fixed?

If you've answered "no" to all the questions, I'll ask you one more question: What are you waiting for? Remember, this is not a dress rehearsal, THIS IS IT!

If you're afraid of something going wrong, that your vanity will cost you a permanent physical disfigurement, don't be—everyone has the same fear, and the chance of anything bad happening is so remote it's almost nonexistent.

If it's money you're worried about, you can almost forget that too. No one said you had to get it done tomorrow, did they? If you decided to go to Europe on your vacation, could you take the time off, pay for your ticket and a two-week stay tomorrow? Just as you'd save and plan for a vacation, do the same for this. Also, you might check to see if you could use your credit card or get it financed, or see if it's covered by your medical insurance or if it's an income tax medical deduction.

Perhaps it will take you a few months or possibly even a year or two to save enough money, but it doesn't matter—because an amazing phenomenon will occur. Once you've *made the decision,* once you've set getting it done as a goal, the physical flaw will stop being so important, and you'll be able to get on with the rest of your life. It will stop standing between you and the you you've always dreamed you could and should be.

ACT II   PROPS: Mirror
                                                             Telephone book
                                                              Pencil

When Helene Rochas was young, she considered herself a showcase for her husband and even had a perfume named after her—Madame Rochas. Now she's chairman of the board and has to have the respect a man has.

Marisa Berenson loved the looks of Marlene Dietrich, Vivien Leigh, and Rita Hayworth. Now she emanates the same glamorous look the great stars of the 30s and 40s had.

The people who wear Ralph Lauren clothes don't think of themselves as "fashiony." His look is "American." It's authentic, with a sense of freedom.

We all have a look. A look that tells the world who we are and what we are. It's not an official uniform, but it conveys through identity association what we do, how we think, what we eat, how we spend our leisure time, where we spend our money, our political affiliation—even our religious persuasion. Our look is the reflection of our image, and our image is the reflection of our attitudes. We are the image of a concept.

If you were to go to a casting call for a coffee commercial, you'd find yourself amidst dozens of young "moms and dads," all dressed the same and looking almost alike—clean-cut, pert hair, clean-shaven, wearing plaid shirts with sweaters tied around their shoulders. "If you want to get the part, you've got to dress for it," advises Squire Fridel, author and number-one actor in commercials. "You should always carry extra clothing in your car. You can't wear the same thing to sell business machines as you would to sell soft drinks."

"The first thing I work on with a new client is wardrobe," says image-maker Kristen Brown, an expert at getting the point across. Her company, On Camera, is perhaps foremost in its field: grooming for the talk-show circuit. The majority of her clients are politicians and authors. She preps them on their looks, as well as their techniques of expression. "Television doesn't give you much time. You can't get your point across, and you can't be effective, if your look isn't compatible with your objective," she claims.

And all the old cliché rules apply: three-piece suits for politicians, the cloth for the clergy, dark colors to project power. I don't have to go into them all. Almost every fashion magazine has an article on the subject: "Dressing for Success," "Power Dressing." They go on and on.

"But the real phenomenon," Kristen continues, "is in the development of the expression of the sense of self, the more dynamic an image a person begins to project with a change or modification in clothing. Their sense of self is often strengthened with this external image identification. They become their own role model."

Sound reasonable? Think back to when you were a child, playing with your doll, and you dressed up in your mother's clothes. The child and her doll were immediately transformed into a mommy and her baby. What happens to people at costume parties?

If you were to paint your face white, draw on big red lips, and don polka-dot trousers, you'd probably be as zany as any other clown at Ringling Brothers Circus, a far cry from the conservative bank teller you are Monday through Friday.

Do your clothes become you, or DO YOU BECOME YOUR CLOTHES? Think of how different you feel when you're in evening clothes. Don't you feel more elegant in a silk dress than you do in a wool sweater and skirt? And fellas, don't you stand a little straighter in pressed trousers than when you're wearing blue jeans?

DOES THE PERSON MAKE THE CLOTHES, OR DO THE CLOTHES MAKE THE PERSON?

> I have to look the way I choose to look, and this is what I choose. It makes me different, a little bit, and ain't that what we all want to do—be different? . . . You've got to have a gimmick. You've got to have something that will catch the eye and hold the attention of the public. But the funny thing is no matter how much I try new stuff, I wind up looking the same.
>
> —Dolly Parton

I wonder what would happen if she put on an Anne Klein suit?

Actions speak louder than words. What are you telling the world?

"The worst part about having gained so much weight," says textile manufacturer Joan Weisberger, "is that I'm telling people I'm someone I'm not. Or rather, I'm *not* telling people who I really am. I have to wear clothes that make me look old-fashioned, behind the times, out of date. Like I'm not with it. Well, that certainly isn't me."

WE BECOME WHO WE THINK WE ARE. Are you who you really want to be?

> Clothes are an attitude. They should represent how you feel about yourself. . . . I've always taken to men's clothes—jackets, hats, shirts, ties, vests, wristwatches. . . .
>
> —Raquel Welch

All the world sees is what we show them. ARE YOU TELLING THE WORLD WHO YOU REALLY ARE?

THE STYLE-SETTING SYNONYMEES
(A WHO-IS-WHAT AND WHAT-WHO-WEARS-WHERE-
AND-WHEN GUIDE)

The Style-setting Synonymees Guide is a guide to image identification. There are many styles of dressing, and each individual style is adopted by people who, like birds of a feather flocked together, have the same lifestyles, likes, dislikes, philosophies, and heritage. Each group delivers its own message of individuality. There is no right or wrong. No group is better than the other. They just are the way they are.

We all have a core identity, a look that is us, that represents who we are. It's our identification mantle. This core identity is not etched in stone but simply a place to come down from, and a place from which we can move when the need, occasion, or whim strikes.

Establishing and transmitting *your* identity, who you are, is your first but certainly not your only concern. Now that you have broadened your scope and you have friends that fill your many needs, they come from various walks of life. As you continue to expand, so will your circle of friends. To enter their worlds, to become one of them and be at one with them, you must be *prepared* to become one of them, even if only temporarily. Your ticket of entry into their world is nothing more than a change of clothes.

For instance, I would dress differently for lunch with Ahmet Ertegun, president of Atlantic Records, than I would for Roger Shelley, Revlon Foundation's president. This clothing variation has much the same effect on my personality as a change of costume has on the actor.

Note: The celebrity identifications are used to create visual images for you. For each Synonymee group, I have given you role models. These celebrities do not necessarily represent the ideology of the Synonymee they are classified as. I've done what is called "typecasting." They *look* the part.

THE BHS (BEVERLY HILLS SWINGER)

CELEBRITY IDENTIFICATION
Heather Locklear, Morgan Fairchild, Tony Danza, Linda Evans, Christie Brinkley, Tom Selleck

WHO
Bright and sunny, the blondes are really blonde, and everybody says "I love you." Affectionate, adoring, demonstrative, and fun. Slim, trim, tan, and carefree. What's the worst that can happen—their 380 SL will break down and run out of gas on the Ventura Freeway, or their house will slide down a cliff and they'll have to stay with a friend in the Valley? Shopping fanatics and health-food fiends— movements get started in Beverly Hills because they move them along. They don't take life too seriously because there's a guru to fix whatever should ail them. They sleep in their jogging suits and live in their tennies except on Fridays, when they put on their hottest gear and it's warm duck salad, a whole lot of kissing—and the best cocktail party in town—lunch at Ma Maison.

Is it the palm trees or the smog that puts the haze—no wait, it's a glow—in their eyes?

It must come from living in PARADISE.

WHAT THEY WEAR WHEN AND WHERE

Men	Women	
		WORK
X	X	Summer never ends, colors know no season— sportsclothes and denim; anything goes, except a business suit. Open those shirts, boys—show off that gold.
		MONDAY-FRIDAY DINNER (formal)
X	X	Something slick you brought back from Europe. The same as always.
		SATURDAY LUNCH (casual)
X	X	Anything from tennis outfits and jogging suits (don't forget to wear your gold) to parachute-silk jumpsuits or a touch of punk.

Men	Women	SATURDAY NIGHT OUT ON THE TOWN
	X	Leathers and suedes, a bit of glitz and sparkle; go European or bring in something from the East (coast, that is: Madison Avenue, to be exact).
X		Open neck, keep showing off that gold. Yes, you can still wear your denims, but put on a jacket. Tie—does he own one? (There are one or two places that might require it.)

SUNDAY LUNCH (formal)

Non-existent

SPORTS (as a spectator or as a participant)

It's a way of life, so they're already dressed for it—and if it's not on their back, it's in the back of their cars.

THE BBB (BROOKS BROTHERS BILLBOARD)

CELEBRITY IDENTIFICATION

Meryl Streep, Timothy Bottoms, Kate Capshaw, the Kennedys, Kevin Kline, Dina Merrill, Glenn Close

WHO

These are the school-tie boys and girls, from the top Ivy League schools. They look as if their ancestors came over on the *Mayflower*; as if they have fathers who were bankers or board chairmen. They cash their checks at private clubs. They like good plain food and drink Scotch. Palm Beach was their winter haunt, but now that Miami has moved north, you'll find them down in the Islands.

WHAT THEY WEAR WHEN AND WHERE

Men	Women	
		WORK
	X	Blue blazer, khaki skirt, foulard scarf, sensible walking shoes.
X		Blue blazer, gray flannel pants, oxford shirt, loafers or wing-tipped cordovans.

		DINNER MONDAY-FRIDAY (formal: if casual, see Saturday lunch)
	X	Two-piece, nondescript, very low-profile stitched-down pleated skirt and blouse (separates that look like a dress), below the knee. Shoes that don't relate, and the purse was an afterthought.
X		Conservative striped suit, solid white or blue-striped shirt.
		SATURDAY LUNCH (casual: if formal see Sunday Lunch)
X	X	Khaki pants, old crew-neck sweater, loafers with run-down heels, fifteen-year-old blazer.
		SATURDAY NIGHT OUT ON THE TOWN
	X	Safe, low-profile nondescript dress and jacket ensemble of silk faille or gabardine. Black patent leather shoes, a strand of real pearls. The bag is once again an afterthought.
X		Conservative striped suit, white shirt, wing-tipped cordovans.
		SUNDAY LUNCH (formal: if casual, see Saturday lunch)
	X	Camel suit, silk blouse, gold chain. As always, the wrong shoes, and they almost forgot to carry a purse.
X		Gray flannel suit, or herringbone tweed jacket and gray flannel pants with a striped shirt.
		SPORTS (as a spectator)
X	X	See Saturday Lunch, but add a hole to the sweater and a cotton turtleneck underneath it.

THE UMMS—THE UPWARDLY MOBILE MAVINS

CELEBRITY IDENTIFICATION
Candice Bergen, Cheryl Tiegs, Bryant Gumbel, Brooke Shields, Richard Dreyfuss, Christopher Reeve, Nick Nolte

WHO
They're into everything, and they dabble in it all; these are the

young professionals. They're well-heeled and well-groomed—it's American designers all the way. The trend-setters, oneupmanship their byword. Their antique family portrait was probably picked up at an auction, but you'll never know for sure because they don't really tell you much about their background. Your basic young intelligentsia—if it weren't for them, gallery openings would go unattended, nouvelle cuisine would go uneaten, and the department stores would have shelves full of pasta machines.

WHAT THEY WEAR WHEN AND WHERE

Men	Women	
		WORK
	X	**Ralph Lauren suit, silk blouse, Cartier wristwatch, Charles Jourdan shoes, Coach or Battaglia handbag.**
X		**Ralph Lauren suit, custom-made white shirt, a good-looking tie, Burburry trench coat, Rolex watch, Gucci briefcase.**
		DINNER MONDAY-FRIDAY (formal: if casual see Saturday lunch)
	X	**Silk two-piece matching separates (either Calvin Klein or Ralph Lauren), something featured in Harper's Bazaar and Vogue.**
X		**Pin-striped suit and vest, Gucci loafers.**
		SATURDAY LUNCH (casual)
	X	**Calvin Klein jacket and pants, silk blouse or cashmere turtleneck sweater, Gucci walking shoes.**
X		**Gray flannel pants, tweed jacket, cashmere turtleneck sweater, loafers.**
		SATURDAY NIGHT OUT ON THE TOWN
	X	**A beautiful silk dinner dress. Although it probably isn't, it looks like an important designer. A bit of flash and dash (Saturday night is her night to really look like and be a woman).**
X		**Dark daytime suit, a white or striped shirt. The tie is**

probably a Hermès, and his shoes are very shined.
SUNDAY LUNCH (formal: if casual see Saturday lunch)

| | X | Pleasant wool dress, or a weekday suit. |
| X | | Gray flannel suit, white shirt, colored silk handkerchief in jacket pocket, striped tie. |

SPORTS (as a spectator)

| | X | Gray wool pants, silk blouse or cashmere turtleneck, blue blazer. |
| X | | Sport jacket with suede patches, lightweight wool pants, wool challis shirt, or cashmere turtleneck. |

SPORTS (as a participant)

| X | X | Everything is very clean, very unwrinkled, brand new, and just right. |

THE IJS (INTERNATIONAL JET SETTER)

CELEBRITY IDENTIFICATION

Joan Collins, Jack Nicholson, Natassia Kinski, Elizabeth Taylor, Tatum O'Neal, Pia Zadora, Mick Jagger, Bianca Jagger

WHO

Sun-tanned, multilingual (well, they can usually get by in French and Italian). Slim, unpredictable, and very affectionate; they kiss everyone they meet—two times. European clothes and European hairstyles (French or Italian). They shop only in boutiques and drive Italian sports cars. White knows no season, it's probably because their heart's "in the south"—of France, that is. The men are rogues, the women love to be ravished, and they're simply never up before 11:00 A.M. They're aficionados of the finest of wines, they eat with their forks in the left and knives in the right (hand, that is). If it's only coffee, not an espresso, then the milk must be warm. They're either very rich, or very amusing. Someone else almost always picks up their tab. Overabundant enthusiasm's the ruler in their world, and they stand out in a crowd, to be sure.

WHAT THEY WEAR AND WHERE

Men	Women	
		WORK
	X	Armani or Ferre suit, lots of leather and suede (skirts or pants), lots of gold jewelry, flat knit sweaters, boots, textured stockings.
X		European cut solid-colored gabardine suits (French or Italian). Important imported silk ties, colored-bodied white-collared shirts, Italian sweaters under jackets.
		DINNER MONDAY-FRIDAY (formal: if casual see Saturday lunch)
	X	Combine work and Saturday night, but leave out the pants.
X		See Work Monday-Friday.
		SATURDAY LUNCH (casual)
	X	Imported French or Italian blue jeans or leather pants and sweater. Lots of jewelry and makeup.
X		Imported French or Italian blue jeans or leather pants, or double-pleated pants and sweater.
		SATURDAY NIGHT OUT ON THE TOWN
X	X	Everything goes—the wilder and more European (French or Italian), the better. Suede and leather, glitz and sparkle, trash and dash. Short, tight, and very expensive; if ever men were to wear silk shirts . . .
		SUNDAY LUNCH (formal: if casual, see Saturday lunch)
X	X	See work.
		SPORTS (as a spectator)
X	X	Imported French or Italian blue jeans and sweaters or white multi-pieced outfits.
		SPORTS (as a participant)
X	X	Cerutti or Fila tennis gear, velour Italian or French ski and après-ski wear.

THE NYC—THE NEW YORK CHIC

CELEBRITY IDENTIFICATION

Cary Grant, John Forsythe, Rex Harrison, Audrey Hepburn, Jackie Kennedy Onassis. I know no one here is very young; but they just aren't making them like this anymore.

WHO

Very proper indeed, they always do things just the way they are supposed to be done. Never too much, and never too little—very conservative, very safe, and always very exhausted. Well, they're always out investigating, and participating, so they can talk about anything. Slim, well-exercised and very adept at makeup; it's only because they look so good that you know they have any on. Very assimilated, you really have to listen to their chitchat to know who is who and what is what. Fashion experts—designers are their thing, but they'll only follow them so far, and it's never beyond the boundaries of style. One must observe proper fashion ethics.

WHAT THEY WEAR AND WHERE

Men	Women	
		WORK
	X	All imported, and all very expensive: Valentino, Chanel, Basile, and Chloe dresses and suits. Maude Frizon shoes, Fendi or Louis Vuitton bag, and a mink coat.
X		Custom suits and blazers, shirts (mainly white), cuffed pants, vests are commonplace and the shoes are Italian.
		DINNER MONDAY-FRIDAY (formal: if casual see Saturday lunch)
	X	Cashmere cardigan set with silk pants or taffeta short skirt or black designer dinner dress. Very dressy detailed silk shirt with satin pants.
X		See "Saturday Night Out On the Town"

		SATURDAY LUNCH (casual)
X		Calvin Klein pantsuit with silk blouse or stunning imported sweater or a jacket from their Monday-Friday suits, with a stunning silk blouse or imported sweater, a Hermès scarf, and leather or suede pants. Mink coat or Fendi jacket.
X		Gray flannel pants or tailored, pressed blue jeans. Blue blazer or old tweed jacket with suede-patched sleeves. Open-neck shirt with turtleneck underneath. Mink or raccoon coat.
		SATURDAY NIGHT OUT ON THE TOWN
X		Good-looking black dinner dress with good pearls. Glitz and sparkle, but only low key and ver-ry elegant from a designer or up-market boutique. And she wouldn't dare step out the door without her mink coat.
X		Dark suit and white shirt.
		SUNDAY LUNCH (formal: if casual see Saturday lunch)
X	X	See work.
		SPORTS (as a spectator)
X	X	Gabardine or flannel pants, cashmere turtleneck sweater, raccoon coat.
		SPORTS (as a participant)
X	X	The proper everything.

THE TTD (TERRIFIC, TRENDY, AND DEADLY)

CELEBRITY IDENTIFICATION

Diana Ross, Elizabeth Ashley, Bette Midler, Cher, Andy Warhol, Michael Jackson, Bo Derek, Prince, Rod Stewart, Grace Jones

WHO

The finders, seekers, and doers. Adventure and danger turn them on. From the crib to Georgia O'Keeffe, creativity's the name of their game. Individuals: avant-garde, electric, eclectic, a touch of it all. They're there first—they discover everything, and they're everywhere. Number One on everyone's list; they make things look like a happening and they always look . . . well, GREAT!

Men	Women	
		WORK
X	X	Far-out leathers and suedes, with far-out silks and sweaters and a lot of good old denim. They never lost their motorcycle jackets or gave away their storm coats. They collect kimonos and depleted the original clothing stock at all the secondhand stores.
		DINNER MONDAY-FRIDAY (formal)
	X	Black dinner dress—but not simple. Flounced skirt, appliquéd stones; one-shoulder numbers—taffeta skirts and knee-length cashmere tunics in hot pink.
X		Oddly enough, a dark suit and a silk shirt and custom tie.
		SATURDAY NIGHT OUT ON THE TOWN
X	X	Anything and everything; you name it and it goes. It might look thrown together, but they've devoted their lives to finding it; in fact they've probably done more shopping and planning of each individual outfit than all the other Synonymees combined. Nothing appears to match, but somehow in motion it all moves and works and goes. Only a TTD could conceive of and get away with a Japanese kimono, a strapless sequined top, silk cuffed pleated pants, and six bright orange plastic bracelets. How many men do you know who can pull that off?
		SATURDAY LUNCH (casual: if formal see Sunday lunch)
	X	Leather pants with open-necked silk blouse to show off their Bulgari gold chain. A Hermès scarf somewhere.
X		Leather pants and cashmere sweater, or work shirt, cowboy boots, blue jeans, and a tweed jacket.
		SUNDAY LUNCH (formal: if casual see Saturday lunch)

X	X	See work
		SPORTS (as a spectator)
X	X	A combination and compilation of Work and Saturday Lunch.
		SPORTS (as a participant)
X	X	Regulation tennis gear—Fila only. For the rest, it's Saturday night out on the town, but . . .

THE MOR—MIDDLE OF THE ROAD

CELEBRITY IDENTIFICATION
Bonnie Franklin, Marcia Mason, Rob Reiner, Woody Allen, Ed Asner, James Coco, Joyce DeWitt, Tom Hanks, Jodi Foster

WHO
They're the average American tourist you're apt to run into abroad. Neat and well-groomed, and a pleasant blend of everything neutral and noncommittal. Never anything too trendy or too much of a statement. Department store shoppers, they're into ready-to-wears, and Gloria Vanderbilt is their guru.

They may not spend a lot of money, or be very high styled, but they still look good. J. C. Penny shopping doesn't mean unstylish. Polyester doesn't have to mean tacky. Some of the chicest women I know wear and travel in only their Diane Ferese dripdrys. Castlebury knits can be stunning. And men, if you're clever, Chess King can turn you into one. A king, that is.

WHAT THEY WEAR AND WHERE

Men	Women	
		SATURDAY NIGHT OUT ON THE TOWN
	X	Conservative little black dress and pearls, matching shoes and bag, little wool coat.
X		A nice suit with a blue shirt.
		SATURDAY LUNCH—CASUAL (if formal See Sunday lunch)
X	X	See Sports as a Spectator (however, the woman

might exchange the nylon parka for a little tweed blazer).

WORK

X   Skirt and sweater coordinates, skirt and silk-blend blouse, knit outfit, wool blend suit with silk-blend sweater.

X   A suit with a blue or white shirt.

SUNDAY LUNCH FORMAL (if casual, see Saturday lunch)

X   Wool dress, or a camel Anne Klein pants suit worn with a silk blouse.

X   Plaid sportscoat and wool blend slacks. A pale blue shirt.

SPORTS AS A SPECTATOR

X   Wool or corduroy slacks, a blouse with a cotton turtleneck underneath, down vest or a nylon parka, shoes—lace-ups or low-heeled walkers with a matching bag.

X   Golf shirt, khakis, and a windbreaker.

SPORTS AS A PARTICIPANT

X   Regulation tennis clothes, nylon warm-up suit (department store sportswear department).

X   Shorts and a golf shirt (but may be regulation, department store or Big S Sporting Goods purchased tennis clothes). Nylon warm-up suit, department or sports shop purchased and/or maybe a sweat suit. A complete collection of hunting, fishing, shooting, and foul-weather gear.

Well, do you spot yourself among the Synonymees? Which group do you think you belong to?

Let's see just how accurate your presentation is. Put on your favorite outfit and really put yourself together—makeup, shave— as if you were going someplace. Once you've finished, look at yourself in the mirror. Do you really look like the person you *think* you are? Is that who you really want to be? Is there another group whose image you find particularly appealing? In any case, I want you to try a few of them on just for size.

Over the next several weeks, one Synonymee at a time, you are going to go to a clothing store and put yourself into a look. A look that is undeniably, classifiably the Style-Setting Synonymee you are trying to emulate until one by one you have experienced them all.

Scene 1. **THE THREE FACES OF EVE**

Objective: To Establish Your Core Identity and Integrate into It
Alternative Looks to Meet Your Expanding Needs

One week before you begin, start testing yourself and your understanding of the different "looks," and component parts. Really look at the people you see, and classify them by their Synonymee group. Browse through the current fashion magazines, checking to see if you can easily spot and categorize the different styles.

Decide at least one day in advance on the store you'll go to. Your choice should have a wide range of up-market clothes. A fine department store will probably be your best bet since they're usually easier to shop in and less intimidating than boutiques.

It is important that you look like "somebody" when you shop, so put on your favorite outfit and be the most *you* you can be. If you look like you mean business, you'll get all the cooperation you need. I'm sure you've noticed that the best-dressed people are the ones who always get all the attention.

When you get to the correct department of your selected store, don't just rush in, only fools do that. Wait in the wings for a few minutes and observe the salespeople in action. Selecting the right salesperson is very important. Look for the friendliest and most helpful. I don't care if you usually just help yourself, salespeople are there to help guide you, and this time you're going to let them. When you begin taking advantage of things nothing will have an advantage over you.

Smiling, approach your salesperson. Describe the look you're trying to achieve and show her (or him) a picture of it (bring a clipping from a fashion magazine). Do a lot of smiling and act helpless. You probably won't be acting, and it brings out the best in the salespeople. And remember, *they* are the experts on this turf so always treat them with respect.

It is important that you get a total tip-to-toe-look, to really experience a whole new and different you. So put together a complete outfit, making sure it not only fits but will someday conceivably fit into your lifestyle.

Study yourself in the mirror. Are you wearing the clothes or are *they* wearing *you?* Are you at ease? Is the sight of the "new you" doing anything for or to your state of mind? Stand back for a moment. Do you like this new look? Go out into the store and ask your salesperson's opinion. Listen, really listen, to what is being said. If she or he is not trying to just sell you something, you'll get a much more accurate evaluation than your own; they won't have any preconceived ideas of who you are or how you should look. Keep the garments on for as long as you can and browse around the store for a while, sneaking up on mirrors so you can catch unplanned-for glimpses of yourself. When you do, try to be aware of how you feel about that person.

Before you take the outfit off, take one last look at yourself inside and out, letting the image and the feelings linger for a minute. File them away in your memory bank for future recall. Put back on the old familiar you and compare. Sure you're more comfortable that way, but that's because it's the more familiar you—for now, anyway. (And you always thought a jacket was a jacket!)

Graciously, with a smile, return the garments neatly to the salesperson. Be a bit oversolicitous when you offer your thanks for their help. Explain that you're not quite sure about the items and you'll probably be back after you've given them a little more thought. Remember, a good salesperson can be of great help in shaping the new you and you want him or her to see the best YOU you can be.

Fill out an I Led Three Lives Lexicon in your workbook for each of the Synonymees as soon as you can. An example follows:

I LED THREE LIVES LEXICON

DATE: _____

STORE: _____

LOOK TRIED: _____

ITEMS TRIED: _____

_____

_____

SALESPERSON'S COMMENTS: _____

_____

_____

WHAT DID YOU THINK: <u>(overall)</u> _____

_____

_____

WHAT DID YOU THINK: <u>(specifics)</u> _____

_____

_____

1.	**Flattering**	yes __	no __
2.	**Wearable**	yes __	no __
3.	**Do-able**	yes __	no __
4.	**Comfortable**	yes __	no __
5.	**Physically you**	yes __	no __
6.	**Philosophically you**	yes __	no __
7.	**Did you like you?**	yes __	no __
8.	**Was it you?**	yes __	no __
9.	**Could it be you?**	yes __	no __
10.	**COULD YOU BE IT?**	yes __	no __

After you've completed your shopping binge and experimented with all seven synonymees, tally the scores. Enter the three that had the most yes replies in the Think Before You Buy thesaurus.

THINK BEFORE YOU BUY THESAURUS

1. _____
2. _____
3. _____

Obviously, these are the three looks that most become you, so prepare to become them. Buy what you can, and save for what you can't. Take the knowledge you've acquired; salvage and try to put together what's in your closet. And always let your YOU shine through, whoever you are.

ACT III	**PROPS:** Tape recorder
	Mirror
	Pencil
	Paper

Though we hate to admit it, it is within the first three minutes of a meeting that the decision is made—we're a hit or a miss, we passed or we failed. First impressions, based on the way we look, dress, and speak, are for the most part the only ones we'll ever have the opportunity to make. According to University of Minnesota professor and author Ellen Berscheid, not only do these impressions never get a chance to be corrected, they set the course for what happens later, should the interaction continue.

Every meeting is a premiere in which you play the starring role in your own life. You've worked on the image you want to convey. Now you have to woo and win your audience with your voice.

And, believe me, you can talk them into anything!

As long as you always remember: IT'S NOT WHAT YOU SAY, IT'S THE WAY YOU SAY IT.

Your voice: it can either be your executioner, or allow you to get away with murder. If you sound like Katharine Hepburn you may be excused for almost anything. However, a vocal replica of Barbra

Streisand except in Brooklyn, without musical accompaniment, would be suspect from the first hello.

In *My Fair Lady*, the idea was put forth that a flower girl can be passed off as a duchess by changing her speech. To affect a position, one need only affect an accent. Right or wrong, or rather right and often wrong, accents evoke an automatic response based on the listener's pre-established images and past associations. For instance, Brooklyn and the Bronx equal tough and uneducated. New York means high-powered, intense, nouveau riche. An English or mid-Atlantic accent signals well-bred, educated in private schools, and nannies. A southern drawl signals lazy, slow, someone to take advantage of. A midwest twang means unsophisticated. Texas flags bigger-than-life excess and lots of money.

Accents can be our most powerful tool in gaining control of a situation, in getting what we want. The more voices you can adapt and adopt, the more powerful you'll become. Always remember, *you* tell the world who you are, and you can become to them whatever you say.

Does anyone hear music when you speak? Is your voice like a rhapsody? How does it sound to you? Have you, in fact, ever listened to it? I mean really listened. If you've ever heard your voice on a tape recorder and you're like most people, you've probably been shocked at its sound. It didn't sound at all like you, did it? Don't chalk it off as a machanical distortion, there are three things that never lie: your bathroom scale, your camera, and your tape recorder. Oh, wait, I forgot—four things—your mother!

The you that you were hearing on the tape is the you that others hear. It sounded different from what you're accustomed to hearing because of the source and your relationship to it. Likewise other ears hear us differently than we hear ourselves.

Our pitch, tone, and intonation are the key factors in what people *hear* us "say." Their effect is even stronger than our accents because the response it evokes is purely emotional. It's not intellectual—it's automatic. There are no words we can say that can change the effect of *how* we say them.

What kind of emotions are you evoking? Are you losing your audience because no one can hear you?

A high shrill voice (a siren) evokes fear and anxiety.
A voice that's too loud creates apprehension.
A deep gravelly voice evokes impending doom and danger.
A bubbly baby voice (Carol Wayne) can be disconcerting, and cause the listener to feel out of sync.
A voice that's too soft creates strain and nervousness.
A nasal voice is grating and makes the listener nervous.

Unless you've studied acting or public speaking, or you've had to overcome a speech impediment, your voice is whatever it is. Because it "came with the territory," your voice is one of those things you just take for granted.

If you've remained in your childhood home town and have a very pronounced local accent, it has probably fallen on deaf ears. And rightly so. If you sound like everyone else, why would you ever notice, or, for that matter, ever want to change? In fact, if you were to speak differently from everyone else, it could even have a detrimental effect—it would turn you into a foreigner and set you apart. Something I'm sure you'd never do intentionally. Even local newscasters now keep their regional accents.

The only time it is essential for you to do something about your accent is if you've left your home town or plan to, and your accent sets you apart by making you stand out too much from everyone else.

But your accent is not our real concern. It's your pitch, tone, and intonation we need to check, to determine if your music is harmonious or cacophonous.

Before you can even begin to learn how to "use" your voice, we'll have to find out if it's even usable as it is, and if it's not, make it so.

THE BEVERLY HILLS STYLE

Scene 1. **THE SOUND OF MUSIC**
Objective: To Turn Your Voice into Just That

I'd like you to read the following excerpt from the award-winning 1951 film *Quo Vadis* aloud five times. Read it very slowly, and try to grasp each word—the meaning, the feeling.

> "Music opens up new worlds, new delights. I can see Olympus, and a breeze blow from the olive fields. And in those moments, I, a God, feel as diminutive as dust."

Now, sitting alone in a quiet place, your tape recorder in hand, read it one more time and record it. Then play it back immediately. If you're not accustomed to hearing your voice on tape, don't be surprised if you don't like it. But believe me, that really is you you're hearing, that's just how you sound. True, the unfamiliar text, the fact that these aren't your words or phrases, and that you're reading, not just talking, have made the focus and concentration different and have caused some slight distortions. None of these, however, have really changed your pitch, tone, or intonation.

But stop worrying about how you sounded and quickly record the excerpt two more times, then listen to all three recordings, beginning with the first. As you can see—or rather hear—they're all quite the same. The third, no doubt, is better, but that's simply because the words have become more familiar, and you're more relaxed. The pitch, tone, and intonation have basically remained unchanged.

Well, now that you've finally *heard* you, what do you think? Would anyone *want* to listen to you? Are you music to your ears?

Fill in your Vocal Harmonic Rating Rhapsody, which follows. You want to be in tune—these are the elements you are striving for, that should describe your voice. That is, if you really want to be heard.

VOCAL HARMONIC RATING RHAPSODY

By: (Fill in your name)
_____

Circle any descriptions of your voice that apply:

IN TUNE	*DISCORDANT*
Vibrant	Monotonous
Energetic	Dull
Clear	Flat
Soothing	Weak
Perfect level	Fuzzy
(not too loud	Hoarse
or too soft)	Harsh
	Breathy
	Wheezy
	Swallowed words
	Nasal

Trying to change poor speaking habits is not easy. Any learned activity, particularly one learned at an early age chiefly by unconscious imitation, has become so permanently embedded that dislodging it will be very difficult. It will require hard work and a lot of patience. You'll really have to apply your DFC (Dedication, Focus, Concentration).

You will probably need a vocal coach to guide you, and this will be a minor expense. I spoke to Robert Perillo, one of New York's leading vocal coaches (NYU and the Stella Adler Conservatory), and despite his stature, Robert charges only $125 for his ten-lesson course. Since New York is the most expensive city in America, I can't imagine that your local expert would charge more—in fact, his or her course will probably cost less. If you need to save for it, then add it to your goals. Meanwhile, if you want to get a head start, or if you want to try on your own, Robert recommends *Voice and the Actor*, a book by Cecely Berry, as an excellent home study guide.

6

Talking Tall

ACT I   PROPS: Pencil
                               Telephone book
                               Money

Well, you look good—you're dressed right, your voice is music to everyone's ears. Now what, if anything, do you have to say for yourself?

The art of conversation: the expression is a dichotomy in itself. It is a complete contradiction. If you look up the word "conversation" in a dictionary, you'll see it defined as an informal talking together. If you were to look up art, you'd find it defined as a skill acquired by experience or study. How can anything informal or spontaneous be a learned skill?

It gets even more confusing because, oddly enough, the word "knack," in bold letters, follows the definition of art. "Knack" means a natural aptitude.

And the truth is that although some of us were born lucky, with the knack, naturally glib—a smooth-talking Cary Grant—most great conversationalists have done or are constantly doing their homework.

> Before each engagement, [Princess] Diana is expected to absorb a fairly detailed verbal and written briefing regarding the persons she will meet and their backgrounds, as well as the history and significance of the occasion. In effect, the princess is constantly in the position of having to cram for official occasions, much as a student might cram for an exam.
>
> —Los Angeles Times Syndicate

**WHEN THAT OLD DEMON INHIBITION
COMES BACK TO HAUNT YOU, IT'S THE
GHOST OF YOUR CARELESSNESS!**

How many charity events have you gone to, not knowing any-thing about the charity? Or political fund raisers, not knowing anything about the candidate? Haven't you ever wondered what a party was for, why it was being given, and who was going to be there? Did you ever think to ask? When the King Tut exhibit came to your town did you look Tut up in the library before you went to the exhibition? Perhaps, if you had, you might have had a little more to talk about when you went to see it.

When the candidate's stance on welfare is the topic of conversa-tion, and you didn't even know that he was running (or that there even was an election for that matter), and you thought you were at a "Save the Blue Whale" fund raiser—no wonder you didn't open your mouth. What could you possibly have to contribute?

To ensure that you'll always have something to say, here's a what-you-need-to-know-about-anything-you're-going-to check-list, and where to find it:

AWARENESS APTITUDINAL ADVISORY

PARTIES
The occasion: who's going to be there, the mode of dress, the culinary happenings (cocktails, hors d'oeuvres, and dinner); if the host and/or hostess are unknown to you, who they are and their interests. Call host/hostess or person who invited you.

EXHIBITS
Museums and galleries—paintings, sculpture, photography. Who's exhibiting: the style of the work, the reputation of the artists, is their work similar to that of other artists'? Call or visit the gallery or museum, check the prior Sunday newspaper or the library.

THE PERFORMING ARTS

Theater, opera, ballet, symphony, rock concert. Who and/or what is playing: the stars and something about them (an anecdote or juicy tidbit of gossip is a plus); is it the original cast; the reviews. See Sunday paper, library, or bookstore for background; auditorium for advanced program. If rock concert, ask a teen, pre-teen, or a punk.

FASHION SHOWS

The designers: their style, their styles compared to their last comparable season; who, if any, famous people wear their clothes. Check current and back-issue fashion magazines, library.

POLITICAL EVENTS

Who it's for, what it's for: are they currently in office; current public opinion; their controversial stands; their popular stands. Check newspapers, library, TV news, local or national political party headquarters, and candidates' headquarters.

MEDICAL BENEFIT/FUND RAISERS

What it's for and its effects if it's a disease; if it's for a hospital or auxiliary foundation, what they do and how they've contributed to the community; the key leaders and important supporters. Call foundation headquarters, check reference section of library.

INTERNATIONAL CAUSES

What the cause is about (i.e. famine relief): what's been done thus far, where does the money go, who are the key leaders; important supporters. Check with cause or foundation's headquarters.

SPORTING EVENTS

Who's playing: league standing, three key players on each team (names and some facts about them); if individual (i.e. tennis or boxing), the individual standings; an amusing anecdote or a bit of juicy gossip about one of the players. Check the daily paper, your library, bookstore, most men.

TRADE SHOWS

If just along for the ride, nothing, if feigning an interest, something—anything—the names of models, improvements and changes from last season's models, visual ability for model identification. Visit product showroom, retail store.

LECTURES

Who is lecturing; background and credits, the subject matter. Call lecture hall or sponsor, visit your library.

DIPLOMATIC GATHERINGS

Who is being honored; what honoree does; politics and history of the country, protocol, something personal about the country (topography, weather, industry). Call consulate, check library and newspapers.

AWARENESS ABSOLUTES: Buy Sunday newspaper and use as a reference for the week. You might even try reading it! Buy your city magazine and keep the copies indefinitely for reference. Learn how to use the library for reference on backgrounds. Become acquainted with bookstores for buying and browsing—often they're quicker than the library for a brief bit of background material. Watch or listen to the early morning talk shows while you're doing your regular routine. Take five-minute "drive breaks"—turn off the rock n' roll and tune in the all-news station. Watch the evening news instead of *I Love Lucy* reruns. Listen to late-night radio talk shows instead of watching scrape-the-bottom-of-the-barrel, where-did-they-dredge-that-one-up-from all-night movies on TV.

Scene 1.
Objective: To Ensure That You Will Always Know the Who,
What, Why, and Where You Are

Until awareness is a part of you, and for at least the next three
months, make an Awareness Aptitudinal Advisory on a 3 x 5 card in
advance of every function you attend. (See example below.)

AWARENESS APTITUDINAL ADVISORY

FUNCTION: _____

WHAT YOU NEED TO KNOW: _____

_____

WHERE YOU'LL FIND IT: _____

_____

WHAT YOU FOUND: _____

IF I BROUGHT BOXING GLOVES TO A TENNIS GAME INSTEAD OF
A RACKET, I'D FEEL REAL INHIBITED. IT WOULD BE SUCH HARD
WORK TO KEEP THE BALL GOING.

Once you have gotten involved in a conversation, whether in a
group or one-to-one, you need to realize that it's not a boxing
match. With the exception of isolated situations, a conversation is
not a challenge in oneupmanship. Stop worrying about what
you're going to say next. Stop thinking ahead. Listen for the period
or the question mark so you will know if you're being told something, or asked something. How can you laugh if you don't hear
the punch line?

A conversation is an oral interaction of ideas—a mind-expand-
ing experience. What a bore you are to yourself and everyone else if
all you ever know is just what you already know. You already have
your point of view, so try listening and growing from someone
else's. Not that theirs will necessarily be valid for you or the final

word, but you'll never know if you don't listen and respond. . . . "Oh, really? How interesting. TELL ME MORE."

Listening, asking questions, and responding are all part of the art of conversation and the most useful tools in the development of the self. These tools will help you to modify, alter, and improve your opinions, adding to what you already know intellectually. Using them will give you new knowledge to add to your repertoire and to use on others. You may even make new friends by letting them be the stars for a while.

Don't worry: giving someone else center stage doesn't mean you're getting upstaged. If the person you're talking with is a good conversationalist, he or she will appreciate that the stage was meant to be shared and in turn will not step on *your* lines. He will also know when it's time to let the spotlight switch back over to his co-star, YOU.

Life is not a one-man show. Always remember, no audience can sit through too many monologues.

STILL STANDING IN THE CORNER, NOT MINGLING—EVEN WITH YOUR NEW CONVERSATIONAL SKILLS? **INHIBITION STRIKES AGAIN.**

How did you look the last time you went somewhere? Were you "party perfect?"

Well, how could you possible use your hands to express yourself with a big chip in your red polish? Of course everyone noticed that missing button on your jacket. How can anyone else possibly find you attractive when you think you look terrible? How can you be at your best when you know you aren't? Did it ever occur to you that your inability to mingle has nothing to do with your conversational skill, that it's your appearance?

EVERY ENGAGEMENT IS A PREMIERE—EVERY ENGAGEMENT COUNTS. YOU'RE ALWAYS ON STAGE—YOU'LL ALWAYS HAVE AN AUDIENCE—YOU'LL ALWAYS SHINE LIKE A STAR

1. IF the moment you accept the invitation:
   - You narrow your clothing choices down to two.
   - You issue the invitation to anyone you want to join you.
   - You make your hair or manicure appointment if you'll be going to a beauty or barber shop. Make the appointment, for at least four days prior to the engagement, if you're going to have a facial, haircut, touch-up, or color change.
   - Oh, and fellas, be sure to order that limo.
2. IF three days prior to the engagement:
   - You make your final decision on clothes.
   - You check to make sure your clothes are wearable; if not, make the necessary arrangements—cleaning, pressing, etc.—or if *you're* the one who must do it, schedule the time between now and twenty-four hours prior to the engagement. Make certain you have all your accessories—stockings, scarf, tie, socks, belt, shoes (do they need a shine?), purse, makeup, hair ornaments, jewelry.
3. IF twenty-four hours prior to engagement:
   - All necessary accessories are in hand (by 8:00 P.M.).
   - Your shoes are shined.
   - All your clothes are clean, wrinkle-free, and ready to wear.
   - Nails are manicured—if not polished, filed and clean. That goes for you too, fellas!
   - Your hair is washed (unless you are accustomed to washing your hair in the morning or you plan to do it just before the engagement).
   - You make a time-allowance card for tomorrow (See Fulfillment Aid #1 in your Showdown Syllabus, page 93).
   - You have not "saved" anything for tomorrow, except tomorrow (you know how things always come up and how you always seem to run out of time).
4. IF on the day of the engagement:
   - You have time to return home to change, make sure you are *all systems go,* and that everything you'll need is right there, ready and waiting for you. If you will not be returning home, make sure before you leave that you have everything with you you'll need: makeup, hair ornaments, jewelry, money, credit cards, extra stockings or pantyhose,

tickets, invitation, the address and phone number of the place you're going.

- You do not go to the dentist or take any new medication (unless of course it's lifesaving—a tranquilizer, unless under doctor's orders, will not be a lifesaver, no matter what you think!).
- You are sure you have left ample cool-down time after your workout. This goes for you, too, girls!

If you think all of this sounds complicated, just wait until you try it. You'll soon see that it's not. In fact, before you know it, all this planning will become as automatic as washing your face. And, believe me, there will be a hush every time YOU enter the room, and you'll own it, because all the world will ever see is what you show them: the very best YOU you can be!

Looking your best, your personal preparation, isn't confined to special events, parties, and strangers. It's all the time. It's everywhere. It's for everyone. It's the Pizza Hut with the gang, a bridge tournament with a chum, or a P.T.A. meeting with your spouse. Until looking your special best becomes as automatic as doing something special to make yourself "party perfect," make a Personal Preparation Propagator Perpetuator on a 3 x 5 card for all the everyday events in your life. Trust me, if you do all this for the next three months, it will become automatic.

PERSONAL PREPARATION PROPAGATOR PERPETUATOR

GOING TO: _____

DATE/DAY: _____

THINGS TO DO (check off when done): _____

ALREADY READY   GET IT READY   GOT IT READY
WEARING: (clothing)

WEARING: (accessories)
   Stockings
   Shoes (which/shined)
   Belt
   Scarf
   Jewelry
   Purse
CHECK WHEN "PARTY PERFECT":
   Hair
   Makeup
   Nails (fingers and toes)

IF YOU'RE TOO **INHIBITED** TO SHAKE SOMEONE'S HAND OR
EVEN SAY HELLO, YOU ASKED FOR IT.

What did you do the last time you were somewhere that food was
served—mingle or eat? Tell me, do you seek out the person with
sauce dripping down his chin? It's not easy telling someone your
name if you have a mouth full of meatballs. Have you ever tried to
shake hands or give a friend a cocktail-party hug with wine in one
hand and a wing in the other (chicken, that is)? With so much
clutter, it would certainly make one out of me (chicken, that is)!

INHIBITION: WHEN YOU TRIP OVER YOUR OWN TWO FEET, IT
PLACES ONE OF THEM IN YOUR MOUTH.

I'd choke on shoe leather too if I thought I was welcome anywhere and blindly rushed up to some people and found myself in
the middle of a discussion about what motel they were about to slip

off to—or an unwanted interloper in a family feud. And I'd probably never leave that inconspicuous place in the corner if I really believed that everyone else is as together-looking as they first appear.

Scene 2. **PEOPLE SOUP**
Objective: To Develop Powers of Observation to Improve Your
            Ability to Assess People

Winding up with your foot in your mouth will become a rare occurrence once you've improved your ability to observe and assess people. People awareness will also make you aware of certain negative elements in human behavior that you possess and would like to get rid of, as well as point out many positive qualities you might like to assimilate.

Start really looking at people. Observe a woman alone, a man alone, a man and a woman together, two men or two women together, groups of people. Notice personal appearances and props and what they tell you about what that person does. For example, take a man in a business suit who is carrying a briefcase and reading *American Banker*. The obvious conclusion would be that he is a businessman and his business is probably banking. Do you think he is an executive? An important one or a minor one? There are many clues: Are his clothes expensive or moderately priced? Are they new or old? Is he wearing any jewelry? Does it look expensive? Is his hair styled or does he just have an ordinary haircut? Does he have an air of self-importance? Is his manner tentative or authoritative? If he is with people, what are they like and does he appear to be the leader?

Deductive Observation will lead you to many conclusions that you will soon discover are often correct. By stretching your perceptions you become more responsive to your surroundings and more effective in your interactions with people.

We wear our life stories; so, as you observe, ask yourself how this person is relating to his body and surroundings and to other people. Does he seem self-assured or self-conscious? Notice how he points up any areas of potential self-consciousness: how the short person may stand very tall, how a tall person may slump. Notice how a person with bad teeth keeps his upper lip very stiff and doesn't smile, or how he holds his hand in front of his mouth. Notice a defensive, frightened person—his arms are folded in front of his chest, and his shoulders are hunched over. Observe the angry, hostile person—the person with his chin jutting out and hands balled into fists. Or the one with the bad complexion who barely moves his head. The schlemiel who just sort of schlumps along. Remember, be aware of yourself and any similar physical behavior you have. If you see it in others, they see it in you!

One word of caution: not only do people not like to be stared at, they act differently when they know someone is watching. Try to be as unobtrusive as possible.

THE OBSERVATORY

THE WHO AND WHAT you should be looking for when you are at something and WHY guide

When you enter a room:
STOP—LOOK—LISTEN
then ask yourself

What kind of a crowd is it? Serious, and intellectual? What type of music are you hearing? Is the crowd quiet, heads somewhat lowered and nodding, eyebrows knitted together, eyes squinted and few big smiles? Are people carefully holding their drinks, and restrained in their physical movements? You'll need to be high-brow and subdued in your conversations.

Or is it lighthearted? Can your conversation be easier—more casual? Listen—is there a buzz in the air, is it noisy, do you hear clinking glasses, the ring of laughter? Are the eyes darting and dancing around, scanning the room—heads thrown back with lots of teeth showing? Is there physical movement, expressive hands, shoulder-grasping, back-patting, casual hugs, and up-tempo music?

Then OBSERVE

The environment—your surroundings, the decor, the art, the colors. Find a conversation piece.

Take a few deep breaths, stand up straight, smile, get a drink, and

1. LOOK for the host and/or hostess—they'll supply instant introductions.
2. LOOK for friendly faces—someone, anyone that you know, no matter how remote the acquaintance may be. If you barely know them, be sure to reintroduce yourself and remind them how they know you. This will also serve as your introduction to any people they happen to be talking to. They will be another source of instant introductions and people you'll be able to come back to.
3. LOOK for an individual who looks accepting and easy to talk to, someone you'll be able to use as a refuge, a person to return to when you need a port in the storm or a place to hang your hat. This will be a person with whom you will feel instant, eyeball simpatico.
4. LOOK for an octogenarian—one of the best choices to get you walking and talking. Generally unintimidating, they'll probably have the best stories, be the most amusing, and know the greatest number of people to introduce you to.
5. If you're single and on the prowl, LOOK for a person you find attractive.

Take a walk around,
browse, mingle,
and
observe:

1. People's habits: what they're eating, what they're drinking, are they smoking? Great for conversation: "I see you're into health food." "Have you noticed almost no one's smoking—have you ever been a smoker?" "I barely see a soul drinking a mixed drink—it certainly looks as if wine has cornered the market." "What interesting hors d'oeuvres—I see you've selected only the all-vegetable ones. Are you vegetarian?"
2. The dress—compare yours. Was your choice a good one? If not, why not? Don't let a bad choice intimidate you. You can't do anything about it now. Just take what you've learned and use it for next time.
3. The age and stage of the people there. Is it a married or a single crowd? You can generally tell, but if your intuition fails you, look for the rings. Don't set up antagonisms. If it's a married crowd steer clear of members of the opposite sex.

Ask yourself:

Do you want to be here, do you belong here, is it what you had anticipated?

If not, and you left:

Where would you go, and what would you do? Then ask yourself, would wherever you go be more enriching, exciting, more emotionally or intellectually stimulating?

If no:

Relax, have fun, listen, and learn. You're already here, so experience it and grow and . . .

Eavesdrop:

Is anyone talking about something that's interesting, something that you know you can talk about? Then stop and drop in and stay for a chat.

Seek out:

1. People you recognize, people you don't know but would like to meet.
2. People you recognize and don't know, but who could help you professionally.
3. People you recognize and don't know, but who could help you socially.

Scene 3. **NOW YOU SEE IT**

Objective: To Develop Your Powers of Observation for Personal Enrichment, Conversational Topics, and to Enhance Your Perceptional Abilities

Put this book down, and look straight ahead for a few seconds. What were you looking at—or rather, what did you see? If you're like most people you probably didn't focus on or see anything. You probably didn't even notice the colors or textures of any of the objects in front of you.

Now, let's try it again—only this time *really* observe; focus all your attention on really seeing what's before you. After you've spent five minutes observing, fill in the Observatory form.

THE OBSERVATORY

I WAS LOOKING AT _____ WHERE _____
I SAW _____ _____ _____
(the 2nd time) _____ _____ _____
I SAW _____ _____ _____
(the 1st time) _____ _____ _____
TOPICS OF
CONVERSATION _____ _____ _____
DISCOVERED _____ _____ _____

If you casually practice this at some point each day, you'll find that in no time at all you'll have an improved awareness of your surroundings. Your observation awareness will add to your ability to converse.

Scene 4. **INFORMATION PLEASE**
Objective: To Develop the Skill of Asking Questions

How many times have you asked your companions how they liked the television show you just watched or the movie you just saw? More often than not their reply was a very simple one—they liked it, or they didn't. If you tried to probe further, they probably shrugged their shoulders, repeated their original response, and never really told you how they felt about it.

The advantage of being able to ask questions skillfully is far more than adding to your bank of knowledge or encouraging other people to talk. Learning how someone else feels is also one of the best ways to learn who they are. Begin with something simple and allow your Probe Sophistication to develop. And soon, like so many of the other new abilities you are acquiring, it will become as natural as driving your car.

The next few times you find yourself watching TV or at the movies with someone, ask them, "What do you think."

A typical Probe might go something like this:

YOU: How did you like the movie?
THEY: It was terrific.
YOU: What was terrific about it?
THEY: It was just real good.
YOU: What was so good about it—*why* do you think it was good?
THEY: It was lighthearted and humorous.
YOU: I agree, but how did that make it terrific?
THEY: I didn't have to sit for an hour and twenty-five minutes and have to try and figure it out—you know, its social ramifications and all that other intellectual mumbo-jumbo.

> YOU: Oh. Don't you like heavy movies, you know, the kind with a meaning? Don't you think we need them, that they're important to our intellectual growth and social advancement?
>
> THEY: Sure, sometimes, but don't we have enough problems, can't we just escape and have fun?

From a simple "What did you think?" you've developed a topic of conversation and enhanced your knowledge of the person with whom you are conversing.

Your Probe Sophisticator sheet will be most effective for you if you fill it in immediately after a Probe.

PROBE SOPHISTICATOR SHEET

WHO _____ WHERE _____ WHAT ABOUT _____

ORIGINAL QUESTION _____

PATH OF THE PROBE (where it went) _____

_____

_____

_____

WHAT I LEARNED _____

Scene 5. **GO INTO YOUR DANCE**

Objective: To Develop the Skill of Getting People to Talk About Themselves—or How to Acquire the Reputation of Being the Most Entertaining Person Around

Your pillar of strength, your knowledge will be conversation to fall back on when there is a lull in the music. But your immediate lure really lies not in your brain power but rather in your ability to amuse and entertain other people with yourself, or with *themselves.* Enthrall, enrapture, captivate, and ensnare them with THEM. No one can do it better.

Talk to people about themselves, and they will listen for hours.

—Disraeli

Using all the techniques you've been learning, attempt to achieve the following four points in all your conversations: 1) Get the other person to brag about him/herself. 2) Admire something about that person. 3) Compliment him on something. 4) Talk about something that you know interests him. If you mentally keep track of your success rate you will only improve.

Once again, allow me to remind you *not* to talk about yourself unless you are asked. Come on, don't you already know all about whatever it is you'd say? Won't it be fun to learn something new?

THE NO-NO NEWS

HOOF-IN-MOUTH DISEASE CAN BE AVOIDED

Long-term conversational studies have proven that one can avoid the life-threatening side effect of chewing shoe leather—disdain—if established conversational etiquette is followed.

1. Don't ask, "What do you do?"
2. Never comment on the quality of anyone or anything unless you know the person you're talking to's relationship to it or them.
3. Respect the confidence of the past. No old war stories please. Boyfriends, former jobs, and employers come back to haunt you.
4. Don't dump—no sinking into self-pity.
5. Don't ask teenagers about drugs.
6. Don't bite off more than you can chew—choking makes conversation difficult and often occurs if you feign interest and ask "knowledgeable" questions when you really know nothing about the subject.
7. Don't ask a professional person his professional opinion.

8. If you're opposed to his or her point of view, don't politic with a politician. You'll lose.
9. Neutrality is the key when talking to the newly bereaved. Don't dwell on death beyond an expression of sympathy.
10. Don't tell an author you haven't read her book.
11. Don't talk to minorities about their minority.
12. No punching back—don't fight with fighters. Don't discuss disability with the disabled.
13. Reject rehashing your rebirth. No preaching or converting. Keep it casual.
14. If you know someone's sensitive, no probing please.
15. Admonishing means asking for trouble.
16. Feigning knowledge of a foreign language is a risky business.
17. Asking celebrities who they are creates a draft. If in doubt, don't ask.

ACT II   PROPS: Other people

If a little knowledge is a dangerous thing, it may also take you a long way. If you're lucky, it will be all the way to the top.

> Knowledge is the only instrument of power that is not subject to diminishing returns.
>
> —J.M. Clark

One of the arts of conversation is being able to convey the idea that you are well-informed even if you're not. It's being able to participate in any conversation come what may. And you can indeed talk about anything, provided you have a few basic facts. For instance, you can easily join in a discussion about a book without having read it, provided you have read the flyleaf or the reviews. You will have almost sufficient knowledge to discuss practically anything newsworthy without ever thoroughly reading the newspaper if you make a daily practice of reading the "News in Brief" section that appears in most major newspapers.

But a little knowledge can also be an embarrassing thing, as I discovered at a dinner party in England. My date, a well-known lord in the English literary world, was leading a discussion of the Margaret Thatcher election. I was daydreaming, barely listening, remembering instead an enchanting evening I had spent with an important man in Maggie's world. The man, reputed to be her right hand, had, under the influence of a bit too much champagne, made me privy to many juicy tidbits. Oblivious to the fact that the conversation now taking place was out of my league, I mused to myself about those juicy tidbits and Mrs. Thatcher as I waited to interrupt with a story that I felt would not be considered too "cheeky." As soon as there was a pause, with a knowing smirk, I piped in, "Oh, so she's decided to run, has she. . . ." The room became so quiet, you could have heard a Brussels sprout roll; shock was evident on every face. My date cleared his throat. "Ah . . . Judy," he said, very slowly, "the election is tomorrow."

My smirk was quickly replaced with a sick smile and a nervous giggle. To my relief, I was saved by the butler, who appeared on my left, serving the main course. They said it was grouse, but I could've sworn it was crow.

Scene 1. **COME FILL THE CUP**

Objective: To Begin Accumulating Enough Knowledge and Data to Form Opinions on Current Events and Topical Conversation Pieces

Your success is important to me; heaven knows this show needs a star, and I don't want anyone or anything ever to embarrass you—especially if it can be avoided, and particularly if it's easy to avoid with a little knowledge. In order for you to be able to respond to a

"... and what do you think?" you'd better have an opinion or two of your own.

Select one topic from each of the four columns:

Golf	World Situation	China	Classical Music/
Tennis	U.S. Policitics	Europe	Opera/Ballet
Sailing	Economics	European Travel	Vacations/Resorts
Baseball	Soviet Union	Art	

In the next three weeks do some research on the topics you selected. On 3x5 cards list the five most interesting things you find out about each. Continue to add to that list whenever you learn anything additional. You'll be surprised at how soon you'll become an expert on the subject now that you're aware of it.

Beverly Hills people have often been accused of not being very intellectual. So if all of this is a bit too heavy and you want to talk Beverly Hills Style, you'll take a cue from the King of Talkers, Beverly Hills's own Norm Crosby.

I asked Norm how he felt about the economy. "The economy," he said, "affects everyone. I know a couple—she's a manicurist, and he's a dentist—and they're living hand to mouth."

Then I asked him about world politics. "World politics are scary. I read in this morning's paper that the American ambassador to Afghanistan was stoned last night. Hey, if I had to live over there I'd get stoned every night, too."

He brought up the classics on his own. "I love Shakespeare, I buy all his books the minute they come out. Elizabeth Barrett Browning wrote, 'How do I love thee, let me count the ways . . .' and she counted all the ways, and they banned the book!"

"Tell me, Norm," I said. "What about exercise?"

"Working out is fabulous, I just joined a health club in Beverly Hills that is so exclusive they only concentrate on certain parts of the body . . . like where you keep your wallet. Exercise does improve your sex life. . . . The second day that I was there, one of the weight lifters asked me out."

We chatted a few more minutes, and then he had to run—he was on his way to Las Vegas for an engagement at the Riviera. He left me with a bit of advice: "Do you realize that when you go before a jury today, you are putting your fate in the hands of twelve people who weren't smart enough to get out of jury duty?"

ACT III   PROPS: Other people

Your conversations with other people can be a very important means of gathering knowledge, if you learn how to use them (the people, their opinions, and the facts). If you combine what you learn from them with what you already know, and then use it all in a forthcoming conversation, if you'll keep building from one conversation to the next, you will soon have a mountain where once stood a molehill.

Cindy, my assistant, and I often used the following technique to learn about the cities we were in during the two years we traveled around the world. Not only did it help alleviate the tediousness of whistle-stop travel, it helped me to understand better the patterns and eating habits of the local inhabitants as well as to ingratiate myself with my many hosts along the way. You see, regardless of who you are, or what you've done, or how big a celebrity you may be, people worldwide prefer talking about the three things dearest to them: themselves, their families, and, be it ever so humble, their homes. This is a particularly valuable tool for the traveling business person.

Scene 1. **THE SPY THAT CAME IN FROM THE COLD**
Objective: To Develop the Skill of Combining, Building, and Utilizing the Information You Receive from Other People

At some point within the next three weeks I want you to go to a highly populated area in your city or town and find out as much as you can about any one thing there that you know nothing about. If you happen to be traveling out of your city, all the better. Sound confusing? Wait—I'll explain with an example:

There you are, stepping off the plane in Miami, Florida. You've never been there, and you don't know anything about the city. You've been sent there for a fairly high-level company meeting. There will also be a luncheon involved, and you'll be expected to make social chitchat, as well as conduct business. It's a great opportunity for you to be discovered—to be noticed by those who really matter. You get your luggage and line up for a taxi. The dispatcher smiles, and you see an opening for a quick lesson:

"My goodness, I'm amazed at the size of this airport—why is it so big?" As far as you knew, Miami was basically a resort city.

"Little lady," the dispatcher replies, "this is the stopover point to South America, and now we have a lot of flights to Europe."

You think to yourself, this must be a real crossroads for the South American traveler. You wonder if that means that there are many South Americans actually in Miami, and how the airport ranks in size with other airports. As the cab pulls up, you turn to the dispatcher and ask him if he knows.

"I think it's either the third or fourth largest in the U.S.," he replies, closing the door.

As you settle back in your next classroom, the cab, you think to yourself, there must be a lot more than suntans going on in Miami. Your next teacher, the cab driver, turns to you and asks you where you're going. His Spanish accent sparks your curiosity about the number of Latin Americans in Miami.

You comment, "There seems to be a high percentage of Spanish-speaking people here, do you know what the percentage is over-all?" You learn that Miami is 65 percent Latino, that only half are South American, the rest Cuban. You recall the Mariel Boat Lift and realize how much it must have affected Miami—you wonder in what areas the effect was most strongly felt. A good topic of conversation for lunch!

There are so many ways to become knowledgeable, ways that require little effort but will reward you with many benefits. Ways that will provide you with many hours of entertainment.

7

Twinkle Twinkle,
Little Star

Well, the curtain is going up, and you're about to leave the sheltered world of the student. The new you, the you we have worked so hard at developing, has emerged. You're about to put all of those carefully acquired skills to the test. You're ready to experience the real world, a world you've known was there all your life but have never lived in. The time is now.

This wonderful life that you're about to lead is like a smorgasbord—a delicious array of succulent taste treats all laid out waiting for you. To begin, what better food for your first taste of life than food for the soul? Food that will awaken your sensitivities and tickle your taste buds. The world of the Arts.

To the uninitiated, museums, concert halls, opera houses, and even art galleries often appear to be imposing, intimidating, and inhibiting edifices. In reality, they are exactly the opposite. They are there for you to enjoy. Enjoy not necessarily in the sense of "like," because not all cultural happenings will please you, but enjoy by appreciating that they are an important part of your learning process.

ART GALLERIES
You've already gotten the background on the exhibit from your local paper or city magazine, or from the gallery itself, but understanding and appreciating art is learning to use your eyes. Always remember, you don't have to understand art to appreciate it. The beauty is within *you.*

To look at a painting properly, you shouldn't move right up to it. Instead, stand back anywhere from four to ten feet. The larger the painting, the farther back you should be. Move in closely for a moment to examine it for its colors, texture, and brush technique, then move back so you can take it all in again. You might not understand it, but again, you don't have to understand art to appreciate it. When the international art dealer Nell Yperifanos considers a painting, she is more interested in the emotion projected by the artist than the actual content of the painting. Don't linger in front of something if you really don't like it, although you might eavesdrop a bit on what others are saying.

Without being too obvious, notice who's around you—how they look, how they're dressed. Galleries are a good place to meet other people.

At many exhibits, particularly openings, you'll find that the artist is in attendance. He's there to meet you, so take advantage of the opportunity. Simply hold out your hand, smile, and introduce yourself. If you really like an artist's work, say so. If you don't, or if you don't understand it, don't lie and say you did. Just introduce yourself and perhaps say how much you're enjoying the show. Remember, I told you enjoy doesn't always mean like, so it's not really a fib. Well, aren't you enjoying being there, aren't you enjoying how it's adding to your life?

Art gallery conversations are generally about the art, so if someone should start talking to you it will most likely be about the paintings. Answer carefully. Don't pretend to know too much. Unless you're really secure and firmly committed to your opinion, don't offer a negative one. Wouldn't you be embarrassed if you were to say, "Yuck, I think they're awful," and discover that you're talking to the artist or someone who is close to the artist? "Interesting" is a good word to use when you're offering your opinion—it's very, shall we say, noncommittal and probably won't get you into trouble.

Galleries will often offer complimentary beverages, such as coffee, tea, espresso, wine, and, at openings, cheese and/or some other tidbits. Remember, you're there to see the art, not for a free dinner. They are not meant to be a meal.

Since art galleries exist almost everywhere—regardless of how small the town—and don't require a major time commitment, why not try them for an appetizer? Whet your appetite, let them tantalize you into hungering for more.

MUSEUMS

Most museums have information pamphlets available either from the information desk, the ticket seller, or in free-standing displays close to the entrance. These pamphlets include floor plans, important facts about the museum and its exhibits, as well as specific facts and information about any special exhibits, both current and future. There is no rule that says you must see a museum's exhibits in any specific order; you don't have to start on the first floor. If there is something special, something that interests you, go directly to it and move on from there. You'll never get through most museums in one day, so if what you really want to see is at the end, or you save the best for the last, you'll probably never get to it. Or, if you do, you'll be too tired to enjoy and appreciate it fully.

Museums, like galleries, are easy to go to alone without feeling uncomfortable, and they don't require a major time commitment. I'll often pop into one in between doing other things for a little nosh. New York and London are great cities for a quick bite; there's a snack bar everywhere you look.

If food for the soul doesn't quite fill your belly, you'll find a decent lunchroom or restaurant in most museums. Many have members' dining rooms, and if you're lucky enough to go with a member or sponsor of the museum, you'll probably be taken there. I particularly enjoyed having lunch, or I should say dessert, in the members' dining room at the Metropolitan Museum of Art in New York, after dining on a main course of Van Gogh.

THE THEATER

There is theater everywhere, even in your home town, whatever its size. And whether it's a Broadway hit or a local community theater production, it's truly a wonderful experience.

There was a time when people really dressed for the theater.

THE BEVERLY HILLS STYLE

Now, unfortunately, unless it's a special benefit or a theater party, just about anything goes. I hope, however, I never see you arriving in sports clothes. True, it's done, but certainly not by a star! And I might add that it's almost never done in Beverly Hills. Our lifestyle is generally very casual, so we use these somewhat more sophisticated than usual occasions to show off our chic.

Dinner clothes or nice daytime attire are most appropriate. Choose something comfortable, that won't wrinkle. Remember, you'll be sitting down most of the time, and for a long time, but you'll also be walking around at intermission and you'll want to look good. Since you're going to be very close to other people, don't wear strong perfume or aromatic hair sprays. The temperature in theaters tends to be unpredictable: they can be chilly one minute and boiling the next. So bring along a shoulder wrap, a sweater, or an oversize scarf—something that's easy on and off. Checking coats is a real pain, so a coat you can sit on is a perfect choice.

If it's an opening night in New York or Los Angeles, you'll probably see a lot of celebrities. If you're thrilled to see them, if they're favorites of yours, tell them so. I always do, unless, of course, I have to crawl over fourteen people and push through three groups to get to them. Celebrities really do thrive on adoration, so if you admire them, you don't have to be embarrassed to tell them, but don't take up their time beyond paying your respects. Autographs are tricky business, and while I love giving them, as do many celebrities, this can also be intrusive, so don't ask for one unless it's someone superspecial to you. Instead, file the memory of the meeting away in the memory book in your heart. Trust me, if the moment was truly meaningful, it will always be available for instant recall.

If you're going to New York and you have your heart set on seeing the hit (or hits) of the season, order your tickets well in advance, either by mail or by telephone. You can charge them to your credit card. Be prepared: they're expensive. If what you see isn't that important, same day half-price tickets can be purchased from a booth right on The Great White Way—Broadway.

London is the second-best city for theater and the source of many shows that eventually become Broadway hits. London theater is a bit dressier than New York, and although the tickets are also costly, they are by no means as expensive as in New York. They are also difficult to obtain at the last moment, especially for the big hits. So if you're planning a trip to London, either have your travel agent help you, or write ahead to the individual theaters. However, if you do wait until you get there, check with the concierge at your hotel—he usually has a lot of clout.

If you really want "a mouthful," you might investigate the many theater tour packages available for London and New York. They'll include all of the transportation, hotel, theater tickets, and even sightseeing. And when you're in Los Angeles, don't miss our live theater. With so many stage actors moving out here to work in television, it has really taken a giant step forward.

Seeing a live performance on stage is magic. As you watch the performers, as you feel them infiltrating your sensitivities, consider the great Shakespeare quote that opens this book: "All the world is a stage and we are merely players." Understand and appreciate that you are not only a player on stage, you're not only the STAR: you are also the producer and the director of your life. And you and your life can be whoever and whatever you choose. If you get into the habit of facing each day as the performer faces each performance, with limitless unbound energy and with the determination to put on a great performance, believe me, no one and nothing will stand in your way.

OPERA

Opera, like theater, is a mystical, magical experience that becomes all-encompassing. Maybe, if you're as lucky as I was, your first opera will star Placido Domingo and it will be instant love for you too. Otherwise, opera could take a bit of getting used to, as it is truly a unique audio visual experience. Operas run the gamut, from the light and frivolous *Carmen, La Boheme,* and *Madame Butterfly,* to the long and heavy Wagner (definitely not a first-time recommendation).

If you are not familiar with the opera you are going to see, it is essential to get hold of the libretto in advance and to read it. You'll enjoy the opera a lot more if you can understand what's going on.

The opera is a more sophisticated playground than the theater, and so is the dress. Dinner clothes, a dark suit and tie, the little black or cocktail dress are perfect. In New York or in Europe, "black tie" doesn't necessarily mean a special event, so even that is cricket. If it's Monday night at the Met (New York's Metropolitan Opera House) and you're in a box, it will probably be expected, as it is on opening night in London.

Champagne is the traditional opera drink, although coffee, soft drinks, wine, and some sort of sweet will also be available both before the opera begins and during the intermissions.

BALLET

There are many forms of ballet, from the strictly classic to contemporary; all are equally enjoyable. The ballet dancer is truly the quintessence of art in motion. The beauty, the grace . . . words can barely describe the physical sensations of watching a great dancer. It doesn't matter if it's *Swan Lake* or a Martha Graham innovation—it's, well, it's just mesmerizing. Although almost every major city in the United States boasts a ballet company, the best are based in New York.

Dress for the ballet is midway between theater and opera. Again, don't forget to read your program; it will give you scads of background material about both the dancers and the story of the specific ballet you're about to see.

SYMPHONY

If classical music hasn't been your thing, reading the program in advance of each piece is essential. It will tell you the composer's intention, what the music and changes in rhythm are meant to signify, as well as offer information about the conductor and any featured artists.

Dress, like the audience, is conservative; lovely daytime, if you please. The crowd is usually of the "heady" variety, high-brow and quite intellectual, so be sure you know what you're talking about with these folks, or it will definitely mean trouble. Concerts are about listening, need I say more? You'll see, after you've gone to a few, you'll have something to say.

A FEW FINAL HINTS: Always arrive on time for a cultural event. That means being seated when the curtain goes up, and being prepared to sit through *any performance* until an intermission. I don't care how much you hate it, or how bored you are, *stay!* Of course, never rustle papers, talk, open and close noisy objects, or snore. If you're that tired, excuse yourself and go home to bed during the intermission. Next time, get enough sleep the night before an event.

As you're beginning to realize more and more, how you look is crucial, and dress is something you shouldn't take for granted. If you aren't sure about the dress code, ask! No one expects you to be psychic. If you're someone's guest and it isn't specified on the invitation, ask your host or hostess if any special dress is expected.

On those rare occasions when you can't find out, subtlety is your key word. Never, never overdress. This is when the dark suit or the little black dress prove indispensable. Always have them clean and ready to roll. Once you've been in the social swim, you should always be ready to dive right into the water.

Special cultural events are happening all the time, all over the world; so start taking advantage of them. The more you absorb, the more you'll grow. There's more to a vacation than shopping, sightseeing, eating, and lying on the beach. Try making your next holiday a different one and go home taller instead of wider; expanded instead of inflated!

Your assignment: There's only one way to get your feet wet and that's to go into the water. You'll begin to experience the world, as you begin to experience the world of the arts, and you can only go at your own pace. There are no time limits, no questions, and nothing to fill out—except YOU!

8

Parties with Pizazz

In Beverly Hills, the world of the silver screen, the land of fantasy, anything is possible. And Beverly Hills parties are just like everything else we do—bigger and better than life.

I asked Arthur Simon, who is aptly dubbed the Cecil B. DeMille of catering, if it is really possible to simulate any kind of special atmosphere in your own home.

"Not only possible," he replied, "I do it every day."

I should have read his credits. They say it all. He's brought New York at night to Richard Dreyfuss for his wedding reception; made *A Christmas Carol* come alive for Shirley Jones and Marty Ingles; turned Rodeo Drive into Camelot; created an oriental pavilion replete with giant barbecue pits, nightingales, coolies, and Buddhas; transported Bar Mitzvah guests out of the ballroom of a major Beverly Hills hotel into the world of outer space; transformed a frog fanatic's apartment into a frog pond complete with lily pads; launched the movie *The Blue Lagoon* with bare-chested, bronze-painted waiters and had the thousand guests feasting on roast lamb, mahi-mahi, and stir-fried vegetables at tables set on islands of sand under grass shacks. And if you were to talk to any of the guests at his production of "A Night in Paris," they'll swear to you that they must have traveled by mystical jet to the Champs Elysée.

According to Arthur, you don't need a sound stage and you don't have to live in Beverly Hills to become the Cecil B. DeMille of party giving. That is, not if you have imagination, a bit of whimsy, and—here it is again—dedication.

"If you're going to have the best, you've got to start with the best, and be willing to put a lot of thought into it, to really plan and prepare. Preparation is the key to successful party-giving. Every detail must be thought out to the nth degree.

"Themes are really the name of the game," says Arthur. "Colors, countries, holidays, fairy tales, even television shows," he added, describing a recent surprise party in which the guest of honor found herself in a world of "Dynasty"—being entertained, along with some thirty friends, by the entire "Dynasty" cast including her super idol, Joan Collins. All were look-alikes, of course. Posters of the birthday girl, wearing Joan's body, filled the walls; magazines with Joan on the cover—wearing the birthday girl's body—filled the tables. And she had thought, as she approached her daughter's house and was greeted by the paparazzi (who doubled as waiters), that it was just going to be a quiet dinner for four. She should have known something was up when the limousine her husband had hired for the evening appeared.

You can bring Hollywood Boulevard into your living room, make your guests feel like stars, and create a lot of pizazz as well, by cutting them out. Not your guests, silly—the stars. Make stars out of lightweight cardboard, cover them with gold foil, and stick them to the floor with masking tape. As your guests arrive, have their pictures taken (an instant camera would be best) while they're signing their names on the stars, à la Hollywood Boulevard's Celebrity Walk—that famous street where the celebrities sign their names and leave their handprints. And if you really want to make it a star-studded occasion, carry the theme all the way through by having them come dressed as their favorite stars. Whose name do they sign? Both, of course!

Gold foil stars, hung from the ceiling with guests' names written across the front (Arthur used them for the recent Emmy Awards dinner given for the technical nominees), is another easy and fun way of turning your friends into instant stars. If they're anything like those technical winners, this will be a memory they'll cherish. "They [the winners] loved it," reported Arthur. "They clutched their stars as tight as they did their Emmys."

The right lighting makes for an award-winning set—soft pink, of course, because it makes everyone look good, says our expert. But it's the food that will really win you the Oscar.

For a Sylvester Stallone party, Arthur created a giant boxing ring, ropes and all, out of cheese (string, of course). Gracing the center of the ring were two large boxing gloves, carved out of bricks of soft cheese.

The watermelon-carved Rocky, however, couldn't hold a candle to the fruit extravaganza Arthur created for another celebrity party he was hired to cater. It was a party given for me to celebrate the success of my first book. He had cut styrofoam into the shapes of massive pineapples, papayas, and strawberries, and filled them with chunks of the actual fruits themselves.

"Who are the best personal party-givers in town?" I asked, certain that he would name Alan Carr—one of the first to have reproduced a real live disco in his own home. Carr is notorious for his parties and has even thrown one in a jail.

Arthur's choices instead were celebrity interior designer Phyllis Morris and Grace Robbins. Having been to some of their parties, I shouldn't have been that surprised. He went on to explain. "While the ambiance and the food are always winners at their parties, their real magic is people. They have the knack for ferreting out a wide and wonderful assortment of people and putting them together to create a stellar cast. There's nothing cliché or commonplace about their guest lists."

I thought about some of my own guest lists, particularly the ones at my flops, and asked him how to keep a party together if it begins to crumble because of last-minute cancellations.

"If all the other ingredients are there, it shouldn't matter." He went on to tell me about another Emmy Awards dinner, the one given for the performers. A few of whom, upon hearing that they were going to have to sit in the parking lot, chose not to attend. It seems that when they ran out of space in the ballroom of the Century Plaza Hotel, they simply opened the walls (doors), removed the cars, and extended the seating area out into the parking lot. With Arthur's creative touches—and the Ferraris and Lamborghinis gone—no one was even aware that it had been a parking area.

"What about the absent guests, were they missed?" I inquired.

He chuckled and said, "Not by anyone sitting in their seats. It was the prize place to be."

Jackie Applebaum is another of Beverly Hills's famed party-givers—just ask her who gives the best parties in town and she doesn't hesitate for a minute. "Me, of course," she replies without skipping a beat.

Jackie also shrugged off absent guests as a no-problem problem as she told me about a party producer Dino DiLaurentis gave for the Italian Olympics Committee during the 1984 Summer Olympics. The Committee members were the only guests who didn't show up!

"Were they missed?" I asked.

Answering my question with a question, "Missed—with all that terrific food and all those other great guests?"

Jackie agrees with Arthur; the food can make the party. "It creates a mood, carries out a theme, and breaks the ice."

Breaking the ice is why she does a no-silverware lobster party. "Having to use your fingers seems to relax the atmosphere. Ice cream is a real winner." She went on, "You can serve an ultra gourmet meal with elegant sit-down service, but if you have an ice-cream bar, that's where and what they'll prefer to eat."

A real party magician, Jackie has a way of turning old memories into today's fun. When she was forty, she gave herself a Sweet Sixteen party, served hot dogs and pizza, played '50s music, and decorated a "rumpus room" with balloons and blowups of everyone's old yearbook photos. (She had them send their yearbook photos along with the R.S.V.P.'s.) The women, who had received their invitations in their maiden names, came clad in bobby sox and ponytails, and were transported to the party in a big yellow school bus. The meeting place? Where else but Beverly Hills High!

Her invitations are highly valued. Rumor has it that a Beverly Hills financier offered one million dollars to charity to attend her dinner party for Henry Kissinger. Jackie wouldn't admit to his having paid the money, but she did say that he was there.

From the sublime to the ridiculous—from elegant black tie dinners for visiting heads of state, to her annual affair honoring the top chefs in Los Angeles. A stunning array of delicate cream sauces, rich pâtés, warm duck salad for these professionals? No way! It's BBQ chicken, ribs, and all the fixin's prepared by Dr. Holywogly, one of President Johnson's former chefs. There is one touch of elegance for this occasion—each of the honored guests is required to bring a dessert.

"What's the worst thing a guest can do?" I asked Jackie. She told me about a woman, the wife of a world leader, whom she'll never invite again because of her incessant smoking throughout the meal.

I asked Jackie for one last word of advice. Her reply: "Be a guest at your own party, experience what they experience."

Now, if you want to experience something special and you've got something special to celebrate, there's only one place to do it in Beverly Hills—the Bistro. I asked Casper, the catering manager, why, with so many other chic restaurants in Beverly Hills (Ma Maison, Jimmy's, Chasen's, the Bistro Garden), upstairs at the Bistro is *the place.* Shrugging, he replied, "It's always been our reputation as the special-occasion place, a reputation we've maintained since we opened our doors in 1963." (Seems to me he could have thought of a more exciting reason—like the Bistro's chocolate soufflés.)

And indeed, anyone who is anyone, with anything special to celebrate, has done it at the Bistro, including many a former President, filmstars too numerous to mention, even royalty—from all walks of life . . .

Beverly Hills—the land of dreams come true. . . . Alice Cohen had a dream; she wanted to be a contessa. So she threw herself a very regal party upstairs at the Bistro. She organized the ceremony and, exchanging her flowered tiara for one encrusted with diamonds, was dubbed contessa. A crackerjack party-giver, her much sought-to-go-to do's have their own special flavor, the tastiest being the little gift each guest finds alongside his plate—not the crackerjack variety, I might add!

A party—did you say you want to give a party but all this fancy stuff is a bit too much for you, and besides, you don't live in Beverly Hills? Well, it's easy for you to create a fantasy for your friends, and it doesn't have to be at the Bistro, and you don't have to hire Arthur

Simon or Jackie Applebaum. It doesn't matter if you don't have the knack of a Phyllis Morris or Grace Robbins, or if the people you want to entertain are just your regular Saturday night gang. Trust me. You're only going to have to do one thing to become an award-winning party-giver—and that's cook up a little fun!

And while you're at it, before you go to the stove, write for an entry blank for the "Cook off." (See page 263.)

Cookin' up a little fun

To Begin

HOW TO USE A PARTY RECIPE

The ingredients were chosen because they best suit each recipe. For best results, follow each recipe, using as many of its ingredients as possible. Improvising and deleting will affect the basic flavor.

Always assemble equipment and ingredients with ample time for preparation and attention to detail, being certain the exact flavor is understood in advance.

The appetizers—your invitations—should be sent one month to six weeks in advance. Begin assembling your flavor-enhancers, the props and entertainment, seasonings and spices, as soon as the invitations have been sent. Nonperishable food items should also be purchased at that time. And a Personal Preparation Propagator should be prepared (see chapter 6, page 144). Perishable items should be purchased as far in advance as possible. Timing is your chief concern, as the tendency is to undercook.

Response to the R.S.V.P.'s should be requested fourteen days prior to the party; begin calling the negligent ten days prior to the party.

Plan a trial run of any untested recipes at least one week in advance. This allows ample time for any adjustments.

ASSEMBLING YOUR INGREDIENTS

GUEST LIST: THE "MAIN COURSE"

An interesting and varied assortment will generally have the most flavor, although it can get a bit spicy if attention isn't given to the careful blending of personalities. Particular attention must be given to eliminating any combinations having a tendency to burn when cooked in the same pot. Care should be exercised not to overcrowd.

INVITATIONS: THE "APPETIZERS"

Specialty party stores and/or card shops exist in every town in America, offering a wide variety of commercial invitations to fit almost any theme. Or you can create your own. Children's stores, toy and hobby shops, and the five-and-dime have cut-out books and coloring books for adapting, tracing, and creating your own. It's always more fun to get a unique invitation especially created for the occasion. Ingredients for more-avant-garde invitations can be made from items in supermarkets or specialty stores (see individual recipe), or you might try combining your imagination with your artsy-craftsyness and using scissors, cardboard, foils, and Scotch tape.

You can also be creative with the delivery of your invitations. For example, if you've created something too large or not suitable for the standard mailbox, and the expense of purchasing a special mailing container is prohibitive, you have a lot of options. You don't have to be quite as show-biz as Stacy (Mrs. Henry "The Fonz") Winkler, who is known for her elaborate invitations. She recently summoned guests to a Hollywood party by writing messages on the sides of pumpkins, wrapping them in ribbons, and having them delivered by a chauffeur in a ghost costume. You can do something similar but for a lot less money by either delivering them yourself or hiring a bicycle-riding youngster, a car-driving teen, or a messenger service.

THE MENU
Actual food recipes are not in this book. You will find them all in any good cookbook. A specialty ethnic cookbook is your best source for any ethnic recipes.

ENTERTAINMENT: THE "SPICES"

Use records or cassettes, hire professional or semiprofessional entertainers, or even high-school students. (If you don't know any personally, contact the director of the school band, choir, or drama club.) Professional dancers are easy to come by—as are zealous students, eager to get on stage, and often for a very nominal fee. Contact local professional schools and teachers. An innovation in the party-planning field is the organization that specializes in party entertainment of all kinds. Check your yellow pages or local city magazine. Contact local pet trainers or pet stores for animal rental. For international theme parties, a local travel agent will probably be delighted to attend your party and give a short slide presentation.

PROPS: THE "SEASONINGS"

The props can be either purchased or created. Where? The same places, and in much the same way, as your invitations. Use your imagination and inventiveness. Your set is very important—it is one of the two chief flavor-enhancers. National airlines of the country of the theme and travel agents will generally be able to supply you with travel posters. Try handicraft shops and flea markets for artsy-craftsy things, and book and memorabilia stores for movie posters, which are also available via mail order through movie magazines.

GUEST GIFT OR PARTY FAVORS: THE "GARNI"

The gift itself should direct you to the best place for buying it. Remember, the world and your own creativity are your marketplace.

ASSEMBLING YOUR UTENSILS

HELPERS, HIRED AND OTHERWISE: THE "SERVING PIECES"

THE BARTENDER

Obviously, the more help you can hire the more fun you'll have, but professional hired help is not always possible. Serving and cleaning up are often a welcome change for babysitting teenagers for a nominal fee.

If you're going to hire a professional and can only afford to hire one, the most practical is a bartender, who can be either male or female. This will not only give a touch of elegance to your affair, making it festive and important, it will also provide you with other services. A bartender can make sure no one gets drunk by maintaining some control over the amount of alcohol per drink. (Drunks at a party are no fun; remember, your guests are your responsibility, and if anyone gets drunk you'll either have to arrange for them to be taken home or sober them up before they leave.) The bartender will also answer the door, hang up and hand out coats, and keep the dogs where they belong. Often they will even help with the meal service. And speaking of meal service, glasses as well as plates can be rented.

THE BUTLER

A buffet meal will of course be the easiest and require the least amount of additional help. You can set it up either in advance of first arrivals or in short snatches, without your absence from "the set" becoming apparent.

If there are more than two tables of guests, a sit-down dinner is not practical unless there is someone to serve. One to two tables can be handled by you and a designated friend.* Do not let everyone at the table help. And always remember, you are the hostess, not the maid. You are not to spend the entire meal running back and forth

---

*An essential ingredient to any recipe is a helping friend who understands and is willing to accept the responsibility.

to the kitchen. Sit down, enjoy your guests, and let them enjoy you. This is a dinner party, it's what the evening is all about—everything doesn't have to be served and cleared instantly! There is no rush.

THE DISHWASHER

If you've hired someone, great; if not—no big deal—you've done dishes before, so there's a few more this time. This is the time when that "designated friend" becomes invaluable. After the party, everything should be cleaned up: the kitchen, the party room—it should all be in tiptop shape before you go to sleep, lest you diminish the flavor of the Hangover Helper (see page 182) you'll have for your breakfast the following morning.

THE SERVING OF THE MEAL

THE LOCATION

Don't have more people than you can comfortably accommodate. If you overcrowd, your food won't cook. For a sit-down dinner, the tables do not have to be limited to the main dining area—even hallway space can be utilized. If it is a buffet and it is plate-and-fork food, there must be seating—tables, chairs, or otherwise—for everyone. Finger food requires only standing space. If, however, that finger food is finger-lickin' good, it's all that much "gooder" outdoors, instead of all over your upholstery and carpeting. Care should also be exercised in the planning of large outdoor parties, especially if you have small indoor space. The weatherman may not be on your side; so always have a fall-back plan.

THE MAIN COURSE: THE HOSTESS WITH THE MOSTEST

Everything has been cooked to perfection. The table is set with silver that's been polished and, knowing you've cooked a melt-in-the-mouth meal, you're all smiles, prepared to enjoy every bite. The doorbell has rung—the first guests have arrived. There's a place for their boots and umbrellas, the fireplace is roaring. You feel like a guest, too, as you toast them—and success. You've produced and are now directing an award-winning production.

All kisses and hugs, and not a hint of the nerves, you welcome each new arrival and personally introduce them, clearly enunciating names, being sure always to include some personal data as you match them up with their best possible mates. The camera is rolling, the spirits are flowing (one hour has been allocated for cocktails), the fun is going, and your guests are glowing. All eyes and ears, you circulate . . . always the star, but now also the director. Oops, keep Marsha out of the corner; double-check that the bartender has heeded your instructions . . . that the drinks aren't too strong, that Ralph's not getting blotto, that Marvin washed his mouth out with Ivory, and that your mother isn't telling that same story about how homesick you were at summer camp. Hopefully, Mavis is leaving a few ears intact; Sherman's hands are in his own pocket; Sonja isn't doing her "Days of Our Lives" performance; your mother-in-law isn't emptying ashtrays while people are still smoking; Harry has checked his black book with his wife's mink, and Fred isn't doing his Lenny Bruce imitation.

The producer, the director, the star. You must be everywhere, and there for everyone. Thank goodness you don't have to run to the telephone—it's off the hook. The dogs and the kids have said their hellos and goodbys, and been tucked away. The camera is rolling and you've indeed proven your starhood today!

Congratulations, Cecil.

THE SIDE DISHES (GUEST BEHAVIOR)

1. Always R.S.V.P. within the time period requested.
2. Dress appropriately for the occasion.
3. Arrive on time. Late is not fashionable; early is an imposition, and

your hosts may not be ready for you. If you have an emergency that is going to detain you fifteen minutes beyond the requested arrival time, telephone immediately and insist that they not wait for your arrival before serving dinner.

4. Always offer your help, but don't insist if it's rejected.
5. You are expected to participate . . . be prepared. Circulate, mingle, make conversation; have a few conversational gambits on hand.
6. Don't get drunk. If you feel yourself slurring, immediately switch to soda water.
7. Don't be argumentative.
8. Don't jump on your soapbox.
9. Censor your subject matter—nothing too personal, nothing too political, and don't talk about yourself unless you're asked. No scatological humor, vulgar and embarrassing jokes, damaging and cruel gossip. Never, never insult anyone. Always remember, this is someone else's living room.
10. If you are on a highly specialized diet, tell your hostess in advance and offer to bring your own.
11. Unless it's a very small gathering, and you're very close to the hostess, bringing a gift is inappropriate and only adds confusion. Send flowers or a bread-and-butter gift either the day of the party, or within one week after.
12. A note should always be sent, or a thank-you telephone call made, the day after.

DESSERT: "THE SWEETEST ENDING"

The party's over, it's time to call it a day. Time to change from chic to schlock, back to those old familiar baggies and, though you loathe to face it, your kitchen awaits—but also, I hope, so does your helpmate, be it spouse or that designated friend. You dedicate a silent prayer to the inventor of the dishwasher, particularly if you have one, as you quickly restore order to the site of the recent Demolition Derby . . . "To sleep, perchance to dream?" Not just yet. First, take out those leftovers you just put away and make a little plate of your favorites. Next, pour yourself one last glass of champagne. Relax for a minute, chew the fat, have one last hoot, laugh one more laugh—and last but not least, drink a toast, give a pat.

HANGOVER HELPER (the morning-after pick-me-up)

No early appointments, please! Forget the doctor and the dentist. So what if you miss your exercise class one morning—the world won't come to an end. The children are taken care of, you've arranged not to have to car-pool today, your house is tidy, the dishes were done last night, and you have just one thing to do. Coffee in bed, your ear to the telephone, relive your moment of glory—revel in your success. Take this time to have a good giggle and a gossip with your friends. Luxuriate in their praise as one by one they call in their thanks.

THE RECIPES

THE ROAD TO MOROCCO

INGREDIENTS	MENU
Camel or tent invitations	Hummus
Cushions	Couscous
Sheets	Pita bread
Middle Eastern music	Olives
Camel cutouts	Eggplant salad
Candles	Mint tea
Incense	Baklava
Guest garb: Middle Eastern, sheik, Ali Baba, harem girls	Wine and/or Moroccan beer

Using a light hand, combine the party area with a dash of furniture, removing as much as possible; "Morocco" means floor-sitting. Toss in pillows. Stir in sheets, blend together, and add to ceiling and walls to create a tented effect. Sprinkle with camel cutouts, incense, and candles. Melt Middle-Eastern-garbed guests with Arabic music, and season with a belly dancer. (You, a professional, or a zealous dance studio student.) Serve buffet style—one plate, lap eating. Forks are not traditional but will not detract from basic flavor. Knives are to be omitted. Garnish with an Arabic brass trinket of some sort.

AN AMERICAN IN PARIS

INGREDIENTS
Invitations: Paris scene postcards
           Eiffel Tower cutouts
           French poodle cutouts
           Handwritten note
              attached to a baguette
              or piece of French
              bread
French travel posters
Card tables lined up to create bistro
  effect
Berets
Doggie bag with poodle on the front
Cigarette holders
French maid
Cancan or adagio dancers
French Music: Charles Aznavour,
              Cancan, Adagio
Guests Garb a là French: anything from a Chanel suit to a starving French artist to a cancan girl or an adagio dancer.

MENU
Baguettes of French bread
French cheese (Brie)
Beef Bourguignon or
Coq au vin
French-cut beans
Pommes frites (skinny French
  fries)
French pastries, tarts,
  chocolate mousse
French wines

Blend French travel posters with a bistro-style setting and simmer. Spoon on romantic French music and spice up with a dash of adagio and a dollop of cancan. (Blend an on-the-spot cancan line from the women present or have a prepared mixture composed of several close friends dressed in appropriate costumes.) An adagio duo will definitely add excitement to the flavor. It need not be professional; a reasonable facsimile can be created by you and your spouse or date. Garnish with berets and cigarette holders (welcome items to take home in the poodle bag).

NASHVILLE

INGREDIENTS
Invitations* (see special cooking
    instructions)
Hay—strands or bales
Jugs
Corncob pipes
Square dance and Country and
    Western Music
Square dance band or cassette with
    official caller
Dolly Parton look-alike
Guests garbed à la Tennessee mountain

MENU (see chef's note)
Possum stew
Fried rattlesnake
Gopher bisque
Aunt Sue's sparklin' white
    lightning
Beer in ponies or kegs
Apple pan betty, ginger snaps

In a large mixing bowl combine hay strands or bales with tables covered with red-and-white-checkered tablecloths, jugs of white lightning and Aunt Sue's sparklin'. Garnish with corncob pipes (a lasting memento of a night in hillbilly heaven). Steep with Country and Western music, then toss with hillbillies (your guests) and fry until golden with a square dance band, recorded or live. Increase the flame, taking care not to burn, when adding Dolly Parton look-alike; perk up flavor with a real-to-goodness hayride.

Special Cooking Instructions:
A tasty flavor can be achieved with paper-doll cutouts of anything Country and Western. For added dash, try a semiliterate note on lined white paper, blended with a few strands of hay. Added sharpness can be obtained by having the note sticking out of the opening in an empty beer can.
**Chef's Note:*
Possum stew—beef stew
Fried rattlesnake—fried chicken
Gopher bisque—corn chowder
White lightning—Any grain alcohol in Mason jar labeled "White Lightning"
Aunt Sue's Sparklin' — Korbel Brut Champagne with Aunt Sue's label on bottles

QUEEN OF THE CHARITIES:
"CRÈME DE LA CREME"
When asked the secret of her success, "Queen of the Charities" Aline Franzen, chairwoman of over 300 charity affairs responded, "I always have an exciting theme, and my food is always impeccable no matter how many meals are being served."

YANKEE DOODLE DANDY
(A Red, White, and Blue Party)

INGREDIENTS

Invitations: Anything red, white and blue:
    American flag cutouts
    Plain white paper with stars
All decorations: Red, white, and blue
Balloons
Streamers
American flags
Patriotic music: George M. Cohan and
    John Philip Sousa
Small marching band or band-instrument soloist
Guest garb: red, white, and blue, Dolly Madison, Uncle Sam

MENU* (see chef's note)

Classic cookout
Gourmet U.S.A.
Vanilla ice cream
Strawberries
Blueberries
Cherry pie à la mode

In a large uncovered pot combine colors red, white, and blue only for basic stock. Flavor with balloons, streamers, and flags. Small flags should be used as garni. Gently heat, adding patriotic

---

*Chef's Note:
Cuisine can be as simple as the classic cookout (hamburgers, hot dogs, and all the fixins'), or as elaborate as Gourmet U.S.A. à la Troutbeck, named for the luxurious English-style country inn in Amenia, New York. Their Fourth of July menu combined American cuisine from coast to coast: Red Fish from Louisiana, Long Island Duckling, New York prime beef, Idaho Potatoes, California wines, Florida key lime pie.

music, and bring to a slow boil with horn-playing soloist from local high-school band or marching band of any size. Add patriotic guests garbed in red, white, and blue and serve over a bed of American cuisine.

ROMAN HOLIDAY

INGREDIENTS

Invitations: Handwritten on a piece of the back of empty pasta box (save the pasta inside for the dinner)

Red tablecloths

Chianti bottles with dripping candles (put the chianti in carafes and serve)

Italian travel posters

Italian music: rock n' roll, opera, gondolier

Garlic on string outside the door

Guests garbed à la Italian: from Valentino to Bulgari, Fellini to Coppola, gun moll to gangster to gondolier, the Roman Empire to Italy today

MENUS

Spaghetti and meatballs

Pasta Primavera

Italian bread, bread sticks, garlic bread

Fried Zucchini and Eggplant

Mixed salad

Olives

Veal Tonnato, Osso Buco

Risotto

Chianti wine

Begin by blending red tablecloths with Chianti-bottle candles and stir in Chianti in carafes. Combine with spaghetti and meatballs or pasta primavera, Chianti, and garlic bread. Whip into a large pan containing guests à la Italian and season with Italian music. A basic sauce can be made from the olives, fried zucchini, and eggplant. For a lighter, more subtle flavor, mix a light risotto with osso buco or a Veal Tonnato. A punchy taste will be achieved by producing a Sophia Loren/Gina Lollabrigida look-alike guest. For the richest flavor artfully arrange food buffet style. Garnish with a bulb of garlic from the string outside the door.

THE OSCAR
(Oscar Awards)

INGREDIENTS
Invitations: Handwritten on white paper with photograph of Oscar nominee clipped from newspaper with Oscar ballot enclosed
Movie star poster
Movie magazines—*Variety* and *Hollywood Reporter* scattered around
Theater-style setting—floor or chairs
Television set
Stars on floor, ceiling, and wall
Autograph books
Two Oscar Statues (cardboard replicas covered in gold foil)
Guest Garb: favorite movie star, photographer dressed à la paparazzi

MENU
One-plate fork food:
  Rice with Beef Strogonoff, Veal Stew, or Chicken Curry
Ice-cream bars
Star-shaped cake (batter or ice cream)
Brownies
Popcorn
Wine or beer

In a saucepan combine television set, movie-star-garbed guests, buffet-served one-plate fork food; spread a heavy-handed sauce of stars everywhere and garnish with autograph books for everyone to exchange and sign for lasting memories. Enhance flavor with paparazzi and serve with bowls of hot buttered popcorn.

Immediately toss in two tickets to the local movie theater for the winner of the most correct choices in the most Oscar categories. Whip with the two costume winners, adding the two cardboard Oscars when ready.

CAROL CONNERS'S CALAMITY EN CROUTE
Or Watch that Messy Food
Oscar-winning songwriter Carol "Rocky" Conners almost had to refurnish her new house when sauce and grease from the BBQ ribs and chicken she served covered her furniture and carpets, and lack of sufficient ashtrays made a shambles of her piano—burns were everywhere —at her hotter than hot, star-studded housewarming.

TOP HAT
(A Black and White Black-Tie Affair)

INGREDIENTS

Invitations: Fred Astaire and Ginger Rogers postcards, or top hat cutouts
1940's dance music, or dance band
Dance cards with wrist attachment
White tablecloths: best dishes, silver and crystal
White flower centerpieces
A white rose next to ladies' plates; a white carnation next to men's plates
Champagne glasses

MENU

Baked potatoes with small dabs of caviar
White asparagus
Champagne—French or American
White cheese
Black olives
Black olive and mushroom salad
Black Bean Soup
Veal or chicken (white meat only, served over rice in a cream sauce)
Cauliflower crudités, sour cream and caviar; or hot cauliflower in cream sauce
Fettucini Alfredo or pasta in a cream sauce with truffles
Vanilla ice cream, cheese cake, white cake with whipped cream

Guest garb: formal attire (black or white only)

For that special elegant evening, blend all your best china, silver, and glassware with 1940s music, live or recorded; season with Fred Astaire and Ginger Rogers posters, and glaze with guests in formal attire. Garnish with flowers, place in a mold of dance cards and champagne, and let gel. Serve with choices from an all-black-and-white menu.

9

The Savage Metropolis

We live in a modern jungle, surrounded on all sides by the enemy: taxi drivers, shop clerks, waiters, maitre d's, household help. The enemy? Hardly! These are the people who have the potential to make our lives work. The service people might seem less important in our lives than our banker, stockbroker, lawyer, and doctor, but they are the people who take care of us, who ensure that our lives will run smoothly. And fools that we are, in a desperate attempt to prove our superiority, we fight them. As if sitting up and taking notice means surrender. Surrender? No, just smart! Consider all the areas in which they affect your life. Consider how important they are to it. And most of all, consider acknowledging it. Acknowledging them, appreciating them, and letting them know it.

Look around you; notice the people who seem to get what they want, the ones who get all the service and attention without fighting for it. They aren't sparring with their waiter or maitre d'. They're not scowling as they attract the clerk's attention. They aren't slamming out of a taxi, muttering under their breath. That's because they know how to get other people to do what they want them to do. You see, they don't need ego validation—but they know how important it is, so they give it. They know that the only way you ever get people to do anything is to get them to *want* to do it. And you get them to want to do it by giving them what they want: acknowledgment and appreciation.

It all has to do with ego and the fact that we all want and need to feel important. The less important we are, the stronger our need.

But the struggle for ego gratification is only one catalyst in the

THE BEVERLY HILLS STYLE

creation of hostile interactions. Remember action and reaction? Has it occurred to you that it is you who is directly responsible for whatever reaction you're getting. All cab drivers are not crazy. No, they aren't all animals. All salesclerks aren't stupid and insolent; waiters and maitre d's don't all have an "attitude," they aren't arrogant and condescendingly rude. All maids aren't lazy. But if that's how you're experiencing them, perhaps what you're experiencing is their reaction to you and all the other seemingly important "you's" that came before you. Talk to a cabbie sometime. Why not ask a waitress what it is that people do to make her job more difficult? Observe a salesclerk in a department store during a busy lunch hour—the rudeness and attitude of the typical shopper. Think about the last time you actually worked with your maid and explained exactly how you wanted things done. Then tell me, who's crazy? Who are the animals?

Dignity. Common courtesy. Respect. Attributes that have somehow gotten lost in this not very civilized modern world. Please. Thank you. Would you be so kind? Sorry to be such a bother. Excuse me. How grateful I am . . . words of the past, long forgotten. Gimme, hey you, I want . . . and we push and shove and grab, saving our words of appreciation for our peers, for those people we think are important, and as for the rest—who cares!

Well, they care . . . and they show you, day after day after day as they make your life more and more miserable. It's called self-preservation!

Action, reaction; you have a choice, you can create any reaction you choose. What else could the response to human kindness and courtesy be? Only a rabid dog bites the hand that feeds it. If you yell at a salesclerk, interrupt, or shove to the front, what do you expect—a lovely smile and a polite "yes, madam?" Is that how you react to your children when they're being obnoxious or throwing a tantrum or demanding attention while you're talking on the telephone or relaxing over coffee with a neighbor?

When you're demanding, arrogant, and disdainful to a waiter, when you send him on endless excursions as if he had nothing else to do and no one else to take care of, when you don't acknowledge his presence, do you really expect graciousness and service with a smile? How do you react to your boss when he treats you like a nonentity, when he demands and commands, without considering your time and priorities?

If your husband carried on, yelling all the time and swearing at you for no reason, if he made you the scapegoat for his day, would you laugh and call him "darling?" And, if he did it day after day after day, would you laugh and call anyone darling? Do you think the cab driver has it easy?

The interactions of people close to you are no different from your interactions with service strangers. People are people; and just as you know how to get your way with the people close to you, how to manipulate them, so be it with all the people you encounter. Always remember your energy is a magnet, it draws back whatever you put out.

Observe the people who always seem to get what they want from strangers, those who always get service with a smile. They are the ones you want to emulate. Notice how they make eye contact with their waiter when they talk to him, how pleasant they are. Listen to the clarity with which they express their needs. Eavesdrop on the successful shopper as she talks and empathizes with the salesclerk: "I'm so sorry to interrupt, I can see that you're busy, but if you would be so kind...." How she gets them to sympathize: "Oh dear, it's so very important to me," or "My boss will be in such a rage if I come back empty-handed, he'll probably fire me. Couldn't you please just look a little further?"

Manipulation—big deal. Play the game. As Mary Poppins said, "Just a spoonful of honey makes the medicine go down." Try a sincere smile and a "please" on the butcher when you interrupt him for a quick pound of ground round while he's cutting a filet mignon for a telephone order. Send a plant or some other small token to your hairdresser to ensure that he'll always slip you in for a quick comb-out. Appeal to the need to help; don't demand, just be helpless. Believe me, if you play their game, you'll be the winner! And winning, I might add, is getting what you want. Service with a smile!

Now, I may be preaching nice, nice, nice; but the truth of the matter is, there are going to be occasions when you are going to encounter nut, nut, nut. That not so rare individual who resents, and hates like hell, the fact that he or she is behind the counter, or pumping gas, or behind the wheel, or carrying a tray, or scrubbing toilets, and resents like hell anyone on the other end. You will know when you encounter one of these. Regardless of how nice you are, no matter who you are or how secure you are, there will be nothing you can do to win him over. Don't bother, and don't blame yourself. If you're lucky, they'll take care of you, barely. Let it go at that.

Ignore the obnoxious cab driver, or simply get out. If you have a complaint, ask for the supervisor or seek out another clerk. When you see you aren't getting anywhere, don't waste any further effort with that individual; ask for the boss, call for the manager. In a restaurant, go right to the maitre d'. Don't lose your temper. Anger is an emotional reaction, and how can you have an emotional reaction to someone with whom you're not emotionally involved?

Now, don't get the wrong idea—I'm certainly not telling you to take a refusal sitting down. Certainly if I've been trying to teach you anything, it's how never to take no for an answer. Almost anything you want has got to be worth one added shot. What I don't want you to do, however, is beat your head against a stone wall or ever lose your dignity when dealing with especially difficult people. Try using the word "must." "Must," you see, is much stronger than "have to." "But you don't understand, I *must* have it. . . ." "You *must* find it, I know you have it. . . ."

How far you go in each individual situation will depend on how strong your need is. If it's really important, you may have to do an on-the-spot, all-out, show-stopping performance. . . . That's a performance, not a tantrum . . .

When the bus driver told me that dogs weren't allowed on the bus and refused entry to my two-pound Yorkshire terrier, Treasure, and there was no other way to get from Amenia, New York, to Manhattan, you'd better believe I went into my act. . . .

"But you don't understand," I said, to his "Sorry, lady." "I have to be on a television show, I must get on this bus." He kept saying no, and I kept insisting, repeating over and over, "But I'm on a television show, I must get back to New York tonight." He stood firm, he was a toughie. I resorted to tears as he began to close the doors leaving Treasure and me on the sidewalk. "But my whole career depends on it," I howled. "I'm the guest of honor, NBC will lose millions of dollars, what will they do, the whole show is about me. Please, please, you've got to let me on," I cried, mascara dripping down my cheeks.

Later that evening I was in my apartment, ready and waiting, when my date arrived to pick me up. P.S. I've used this television show ploy many times, and found it particularly effective with airline personnel.

Regardless of how you hate taking no for an answer, the time and energy expended in trying to convert a no into a yes is sometimes not worth the time. Sometimes nothing will do the trick . . .

After spending forty-five minutes in a Manhattan sound store, it finally became apparent to me that the salesman was not going to explain the workings of the telephone-answering machine I had come in to buy. Fool that I was, I had originally thought I could persuade him otherwise. My alloted time for the task had run out, I was going to be late if I didn't wrap it up then and there. I needed the machine, and I needed someone to explain how the machine worked. In desperation, I stamped my foot and said, "I've had quite enough of you, I've never dealt with anyone more impossible—let me see the manager this minute!" My voice had unfortunately reached the glass-shattering twelve-decibel level. The jerk responded with, "I'm the manager, lady." Oh damn, I thought, now what. I had to come back at him with something. Undeterred, I whipped back, barely showing a quiver of eyelash, "Then I'll have to speak to daddy about that! Which one of our stores is this anyway?" And as I walked out, as if to check the street to confirm where I was, I walked smack into the door. Certainly not one of my best exits.

Now, while I did get a good giggle out of it, I almost got a concussion, too; and I never did get my telephone-answering machine. Was it worth it? After all, if you don't get the Oscar then you aren't really a star! The Oscar, in this case, was of course the answering machine.

Well, you can't win them all!

10

The Roar of the Restaurant, the Hush of the Crowd

Restaurants used to be places to go to eat. Today they're where we go to meet, greet, make money, and be seen. Run like exclusive private clubs, some, like Ma Maison in Beverly Hills, even have unlisted telephone numbers. "For members only," or so you'd think if you were to call Lucille Ball's and Cara Williams's favorite Sunday night spaghetti haunt, Matteo's in Westwood, for a seven-thirty reservation. Do you think that just anyone will be seated in the front room at Chasen's or get a table upon arrival at Morton's? Only a handful receive instant attention at Spago's. The rest of us must reserve two weeks in advance and pray that we will be seated something short of two hours after our arrival.

In New York, the same holds true. The first room at Le Cirque, a booth at the Russian Tea Room, same day reservations at Prima Donna without knowing someone, or a front table at Elaine's—these are reserved for the chosen few.

And for what? To be part of an elite, chic, social scene where, quite frankly, the food often ranks a sour second to the glamour. But then, the glamour is what it's all about. Regardless of its size, every city has its powerhouses, where the dues are high and the initiation tough.

Restaurants have also become slick stage settings where everyone plays a carefully rehearsed part. Understanding and playing your role is what will ultimately win you your Oscar—attention and a good table. In this one show, however, you are not the star. In restaurants you are simply the audience. The stars are the maitre d's, the captains, the waiters, yes, even the busboys and the car valets. And, like all other performers, they expect and thrive on their applause and ovations. To them, however, it comes in a slightly different form: respect, good behavior, proper manners, AND handshakes: handshakes that carry a green thank-you along with them.

The *maitre d'* is by far the leading man, seemingly a pompous little partridge ruling his roost, his right hand automatically swings into action with each new arrival and departure. It's this hand that one dares not leave empty for fear of instant reprisal, which means instant nothing—no reservations no table, no service. Instead, a "Sorry, we're booked."

With the lofty air of those "to the manor born," the maitre d's respond best to Mid-Atlantic-accented graciousness. This is particularly useful when making reservations. They turn on when addressed with a "good afternoon" or "good evening," and shine when complimented (perhaps for a boutonniere). If you are there to meet someone, tell the maitre d' so he can escort you into the room. Never, never, plunge in to find your party by yourself.

What do you do if he ignores you; if he lets you stand at the entrance while he talks at length on the telephone; if he wanders through the room chatting with those already seated; or if he looks right through you to welcome a familiar face that arrived after you? Nothing. That's right, absolutely nothing, except perhaps choose not to return. You can't and shouldn't try to show him by withholding or lowering your tip because then the choice of whether or not to return won't be yours; it will already have been made for you. You, unfortunately, always must be the one who is above it all, because a maitre d' will never apologize for his conduct. He will be quick to point out that his capacity is limited, both in seating and attention, and it is completely natural for him to favor his loyal clientele and maintain the standards that made "his" restaurant so popular in the first place. And rightly so. Before you judge him too harshly, stand back for a moment and watch him in action.

Just watch Bruno at Le Cirque, or Fernand at Ma Maison—combination tightrope walker, magician, impresario. Try to imagine him in normal clothing, getting a manicure in a pair of blue jeans and a leather jacket. You see he is a real person, he's only doing his job. The more he keeps you on your toes, the better job he's doing. The happy seated people upon whom he has been showering his attention are his bread and butter; his responsibility is to keep them happy. He knows he can depend on them. You, on the other hand, could be a one-time shot. You might never come back again. Not only that, you might not be the kind of person he'd even want to invite back into his "home." Prove yourself with proper behavior, repeated visits, and generous thank-yous.

A *captain* is a regular breed of chap; well, at least he's civil. He is well aware of his role, and it's not to intimidate you. Don't let the fluency of his forked French tongue throw you as he reels off with the speed of a bullet those Voillettes and Mousses Chauds de Crevettes. It often has nothing to do with his intellectuality but is rather a gift of his birthright. If he's going too fast, slow him down and ask him to repeat himself. If you don't understand what something is, ask. But no barking, please. Always remember to ask graciously.

Notice how his eyes are staring straight ahead? That's not meant to be an attitude—it's not that he's not talking to you. Remember he's an actor, and you're his audience. He's just reciting memorized lines. Remembering lines takes concentration, and if he looked at you he'd be apt to forget them.

All performers, including the captain, thrive on an appreciative, accepting audience. Let this performer know you appreciate him; let him be your friend. After all, he is the one most responsible for what you're going to eat. Should you have special needs, he is the one who will ensure that they'll be met. Oh, and P.S., remember that he's next in line to be maitre d'!

Although all the *waiter* does is serve the food and he is odd-man out in the restaurant triumvirate, he is your way in—into your food, that is: whether it's hot, cold, or even there at all. Never underestimate the importance of his supporting role.

Not even the lowest man on the totem pole, the *busboy*, deserves your disdain. Believe me, he's important too. How else would you get your bread and butter? Who else is going to fill that water glass?

He is the one who will replace your fork when you so carelessly drop it.

In Chapter Two I told you not to worry about what the *valet* thought of you. "After all, he's only the valet," I said. My reference, "only the valet," was in terms of any concerns you might have about his personal assessment of you based on his opinion of the quality of your car. His opinion of you, his reaction to you, like everyone else's *is* important, but it will not be based on the kind of car you drive. He, like everyone else who deals with people with money and power, knows that you can never judge a book by its cover. Some of his biggest tips have come from the most unexpected sources. His opinion of you, his reaction to you? Remember action/reaction? Nice, is nice, is nice—you get more bees with honey . . . and in this case the bee is your car, returned to you quickly and intact.

When going to a new restaurant remind yourself that first times at anything are difficult and especially when it's a restaurant where, as a newcomer, you're on trial and constantly challenged. But the challenge of restaurants, like everything else, will soon become a game, now that you know you belong!

SOUR GRAPES A LA CARTE

A Not So Delectable Array of Restaurant Behavior
Guaranteed to Leave a Bad Taste in the Mouth

Non-Appetizers

Arriving late for a reservation without calling—ten minutes is late.

Arriving early for a reservation and insisting on immediate seating.

Arriving with no reservation and expecting and insisting on service.

Dressing inappropriately—under- or over-. Even the most powerful are challenged.

Being loud and flashing cash at the door.

Being a pest while waiting for your table (if you are asked to wait, ascertain how long the wait will be and do not recheck until the time is up).

Getting drunk at the bar.

Non-Entrees

Holding a lighted cigarette in your hand as you walk to your table.

Lingering excessively long at the table of an acquaintance.

Smoking cigars.

Asking to switch tables and refusing to take no for an answer.

Talking too loudly or using vulgarity.

Calling to friends across the room.

Arguing with your companion.

Being discourteous to neighbors (particularly with regard to smoking).

Treating staff like subordinates.

Using your plate as an ashtray.

Sending your waiter on countless missions.

Sending back food because *you* made a mistake.

Dessert

Lingering too long in a busy restaurant.

Questioning the bill unnecessarily (if the error is under 5 percent, please forget it).

Arguing with your companion about who is going to pay.

Bringing too little money or incorrect credit cards (if it should happen, a quiet discussion with the maitre d' will probably persuade him to accept your personal check).

Undertipping. You should tip 15 to 20 percent of the bill. If there is a captain and a waiter, a quarter of the amount goes to the captain. In addition, the maitre d' should be given between $5 and $20 via a discreet handshake when you are leaving. A pre-seating tip must be done with much discretion and finesse. If you do it, do it with confidence, and never give the impression of its being a bribe—it's an expression of appreciation for services rendered.

THE CHEF RECOMMENDS:

Remember that restaurants are stage sets. It is important to the owners and maitre d's to dress them up. They must have beautiful people as well as celebrities. Physically pleasing people are the first unknowns to be acknowledged. If you do your best with whatever you've got to wear, it should get you better positioning as well as getting you in.

No one wants to be placed in the draft by the entrance, the swinging doors to the kitchen, or the archway leading to the bathrooms. But these tables are reserved for someone, and if you're a first-timer they're reserved for you. It is all right to suggest firmly that the table is simply not acceptable, but if your complaint falls on deaf ears don't try to get them to hear. They won't—and will forever be deaf to the sound of your name. If you ever want to return, grin and bear it, and know that you'll be moved up the line.

If the service is not what it should be, a pointed suggestion to the waiter is in order. But if it is ignored, go directly to the maitre d'. Don't be abrasive, loud, vulgar, argumentative, or whiny. State your case firmly, with dignity, being certain to say, "This is simply not acceptable."

A BIT OF THE BUBBLY

Restaurant Entertaining

Time
If you're going to be late, call the maitre d', have him seat your guests and serve them drinks. If you're the guest, call if you are more than fifteen minutes late, and request that they begin without you.

Seating
The best seats go to the guests. Let them experience the ambiance and the action. If you're the guest, wait until your host/hostess seats you. If no suggestion is made, ask.

Ordering

Unless it's for more than twenty people, no pre-ordered meals. Let your guests experience the fun of restaurants by eating whatever they want. If you're the guest, don't order the most expensive item on the menu.

Problems

The meat too well-done, someone needs more butter? Handle all problems for your guests. If it's anything major, excuse yourself and *go* to the maitre d'—no hassles in front of your guests, please. If you're the guest, don't make a scene; if something isn't right, tell your host or hostess.

Paying

Don't study the bill forever; you should have mentally computed it in advance. Pay quickly, always smiling. If there's a problem, pay the bill and settle the problem after you have escorted your guests out. Cash is class, as is paying in advance. If you are paying by credit card, have them stamp the slip in advance and sign it, adding the appropriate percentage for the tip, or sign it on your way out. If you're the guest, don't stare at your host while he is paying. In fact, look the other way. And don't forget to say thank you *after* the final transaction has taken place and you've started to leave the table.

11

Heaven or Hell

ACT I
The Inn of the Sixth Happiness: Hotels

A high-ranking cosmetic executive who travels extensively took her twelve-year-old stepson on a trip to Paris. As a game, they decided to let him take over and run the show. From the time they left home, he was in charge. A sophisticated traveler himself (he acquired Beverly Hills Style at an early age), he arranged for the car to the airport, took care of the luggage, checked them in, and handled the seating. Although he didn't speak a word of French, he did the same when they arrived in Paris. He got them through Passport Control, picked up their luggage, organized the car, and proudly strode ahead of his stepmother into the Crillon Hotel. His wide grin disappeared, his shoulders slumped. Teary-eyed and defeated, he turned back to her, saying, "Gee, Brenda, I bet you don't even know what to do now!"

And he's not alone. Many well-seasoned adult travelers become confused upon checking into a hotel. Hotel lobbies, while always slightly intimidating, used to be honest and up-front. You knew where you were. Now they're either massive marble rooms with an elaborate array of countless unmarked desks and areas, filled with eye-avoiding bodies clad in tuxedos, or they're massive marbled rooms that are bare save for mirrored walls and elevators hidden somewhere behind the massive potted palms and climbing philodendrons. They are entry points from which your luggage is shuttled from your side as you move on to the next level to check in, wherever that is.

THE BEVERLY HILLS STYLE

Hotel lobbies have become a snare to trap and intimidate you so that the refuge of your room will appear to be a womb of security, its four walls encasing you in comfort. It isn't until hours later, when your luggage finally arrives from somewhere within the hotel's cavernous depths, that you realize there isn't room for both of you—you and your luggage. Toiletries in hand, you step into the bathroom and wonder if there are many casualties in this dimly lit cove with the recessed lighting. There's no room for your own things on the little counter because it's already crowded with an assortment of shoeshine kits, sewing kits, shower caps—and heaven knows the brand of the shampoos, body creams, and deodorants. No hooks for your nightgown and robe; they're already occupied by a variety of bathrobes in various colors and sizes.

Hotels used to direct their attention to the guest. The customer was the star. And yet now, with even more staff than guests, the hotel with the personal welcome, the days of caring all seem gone forever. But the hotels will pay attention to you. All you have to do is ask. If you're willing to take whatever they dish out, learn to like the leftovers. The prime cuts, you see, are reserved for the discerning, for those who ask for, demand, and expect them. They do have better rooms, but if you'll accept the broom closet, as nine out of ten people will, why should they waste a good room on you?

Your key phrase for a room change: "This is simply not acceptable." Once the phrase is uttered, do not unpack your luggage, do not allow anyone to put you off. If your request is denied, ask to be connected to the assistant manager. If that doesn't work, go down and talk to him in person. It takes effort; the management might not give in at first. If they continue to unrelent despite your repeated, "but you don't seem to understand, this is simply unacceptables," and if it is truly unacceptable, and you won't be comfortable, tell them to find you a room that is acceptable somewhere else. Barring a major convention in town, the Beverly Hills Hotel during Academy Award week, or New York City two weeks before Thanksgiving, they'll find you another room in their hotel. Rarely will they resort to sending you elsewhere. They need you tonight. They don't want you to leave. It's unlikely that they'll find anyone else to take your place. You are the reason they're working there.

Don't let the staff's affected air and fancy dress put you off. Remember, although they're on stage, they aren't really actors. Not only are they real people, hotel people are special people; they're goodwill ambassadors and are really there to serve you. Believe me, they want to see you happy, they want to see you satisfied. They like it when you're smiling—it makes them feel good. When you pass by and laugh with them and joke with them and share stories with them, you entertain them. And, if they make you feel happy, you might even augment their meager salaries.

And who are all those busy, official-looking people? What are their individual roles in keeping you happy?

THE MANAGER: Hardly ever to be seen. Unless you've come to him via a personal recommendation or he's a personal friend of yours, he's not an important contact for you to have.

THE ASSISTANT MANAGER: The front-man for the manager, he really runs the show. Trouble-shooter, greeter, VIP welcome wagon, this is the man to know. Butter him up and make him your friend, and he'll insure that while you're in "his home," you're in the lap of luxury. He's the person you'll call for all your future reservations. Compliments and gossip win his heart. He, like all hotel people, is a people-person, and he loves to chitchat. Bored with too much routine, he welcomes bits of scandal to spice up his life. He thrives on having personalities in his house, so let him think you're somebody, and he'll love it. Though he prides himself on being discreet and indeed *some are* (I could never get a word out of Mr. Brown at The Beverly Hills or Mr. Weck at The Regency), some of them love to talk almost as much as they love to listen. Catch a "talker" in the right mood, and OH BOY will you ever get an earful. What a dossier I built up in my three years of hotel living!

Heed my warning: once you've established a relationship with an assistant manager, don't abuse it. Don't call anyone else for your reservation, and heaven forbid if you should ever get careless and cancel one through someone else. Try it, and the next time you try to make a reservation you'll be left out in the cold. I once made that error with Mr. Fernandez, the beloved, now retired, assistant manager of The Regency. I cancelled my reservation through someone else, and my once-close chum barely spoke to me and refused a reservation request the next time I called. After effusive apologies, I was able to worm my way back into his heart and under his roof.

A discreet "green" handshake when you leave and a charming little note once you return home will earn you a place among his circle of friends.

THE CONCIERGE: Your man Friday and every day. Long a European tradition, this recent addition to the basic Americana hotel scene is now found at hotels everywhere. There's almost nothing he can't do for you. Challenges are his pride and joy: airline reservations, theater tickets, a repair if your luggage breaks, sight-seeing tours, a pound of smoked salmon shipped to Fiji, cheesecakes from three different bakeries; he'll even find you a special dog from a special breeder. Introduce yourself, with your name and room number, the moment you arrive. Tip him then and he'll dispense his boys—the bellmen—like bullets from a Gatling gun. Oh, and don't forget to slip him a little more when you leave.

THE BELLMAN: Your information central. He knows everything and anything you need to know or might want to know about the city you're in; the who, what, where, why, and how you do it. Local color and gossip, best restaurants. You name it, he knows it. He works on tips—for you and from you. One dollar per service is customary.

THE CHAMBERMAID: Those nice crisp sheets, those fresh fluffy towels that you never have to pick up, and that little chocolate bonbon on the pillow of your turned-down bed each night are a big part of what's going to make your hotel stay pleasant. A little "stuffed" envelope on that pillow the first morning after your arrival will have the maid there whenever you need her. You know that you aren't confined to a morning and evening visit only. You can call housekeeping whenever you need her; if the room's a bit messy after an afternoon tryst, or you need extra towels or can't get your dress buttoned . . . twenty-four-hours-a-day, just pick up the phone and say "help."

If you know how to use a hotel, being a guest in one can be the closest thing to being queen for a day. Oh, don't forget to thank your maids again when you leave. And you know that a thank-you in hotel talk is spelled m-o-n-e-y.

Now if you really want to be pampered, try pampering the behind-the-scenes people. Whether you're traveling for business or fun, the telephone operator is vital. That is, unless you want to sit and wait for telephone calls. Unfortunately, as any frequent traveler will tell you, the number of misplaced messages and unpaged pages is so staggering one almost has to do just that. Unless, of course, you've insured that the telephone operators know you, and like you, and will make a personal effort to see that you get every one of your calls, no matter where you are.

That same traveling executive who took her son to Paris made the hotel telephone operators her first priority. The first thing she did when she got to her room was call and introduce herself. She followed the call up with a small gift, a cosmetic sample she had with her. From that moment on, she had her own personal secretaries as well as an answering service.

I do something similar with the room service clerks. My food needs are very specific, and I'm quite particular about its preparation. It's hard enough to get my "no salt, please" message across to a waiter when he's giving me his undivided attention, but it's almost impossible with a person answering many telephone calls. That is, unless you send down a little "green" envelope when you first arrive.

If you'll be doing a lot of entertaining in the restaurant, or in any of the hotel's public rooms, be sure you introduce yourself to and take care of the maitre d', even before you go there the first time. If you want a spot held for you at the pool, don't forget the pool-boys.

Although tipping is the best tip I can give you for a successful hotel stay anywhere in the world, don't get nervous about the expense; you won't really need a lot of money. Lots of dollar bills, perhaps, but that's not necessarily lots of dollars.

Equally as important as your money is your good will; in fact it may even be more important. As I said earlier, hotel people are a specific breed; they are truly people-lovers. They love to talk to them, listen to them, respond to them, entertain them, take care of them, and fantasize about them. To them, people are one of life's greatest enjoyments; nice people, charming people, polite people. They like to make a buck, but getting rich is not their goal. It's not the big tipper with the big mouth and condescending attitude who wins their affection. On the contrary, they take his or her money and perform the minimum of service. It's the people who show them a little attention, who win their hearts. These are the people for whom they'll run and do and give their all. You can be one of them, if you do it their way.

VIP carries a lot of weight—in stature, not in size. Whether on the computer printout of a large chain operation or handwritten on the advance registration card of a very prestigious independent, VIP means something. It means personalized service. If a hotel official is alerted in advance of your booking, you won't have to ask for service. It will be automatic. If it's your first visit, don't hesitate to use your friends and acquaintances who have connections to make your reservations for you, or you can use their names if you make them yourself. Rarely do any important people travel to a new place without a personal introduction preceding them. Should it happen, however, they claim nary a problem. Why? Because they look important!

The essence of a fine hotel is the quality of its guests. The more important the hotel thinks you are, the more important you become to them. Important people always look the part. Never, never check into a hotel looking anything but your best. I don't care if you've just gotten off a 22-hour flight and had 12 hours of delays en route. Just like a film star, you must always be ready for the photographers and film crew that will be there to meet your flight. At no other time will you be meeting more people than when you're traveling—especially when you first arrive. IT'S NO TIME TO LOOK LIKE A SLOB! Try it once and notice the greeting you get. When they spy you on the closed-circuit television from the cameras hidden in the climbing philodendrums, they'll know *someone* important has arrived and they'll open their arms to greet you.

DISCOUNTS: They're often available to VIPs, frequent guests, business travelers (corporate rates), airline personnel, and travel agents.

Always ask about them, and be sure to carry your business cards with you. Although I'm certainly not recommending it, I know of some people who pose as travel agents and have even gone so far as to have a business card made up with a travel agency name printed on it. They use that same scam with airlines to try to get upgrades.

UPGRADES: If your room really is terrible, and you really do find it unacceptable, and they do accommodate you by moving you to a better room, you should not be charged more for the better room. Stand your ground; they have created an inconvenience for you, and they should bear the burden of it. Don't, however, expect the Royal Suite if you've reserved a room in the lowest price range. Not even I have been able to pull that one off. It's always good policy to book a room that has a mid-range price. That way, first class isn't too far away.

Hotels—heaven or hell? It's all up to you and what you make them.

ACT II
Waltzing in the Clouds

When you think of travel, you think of adventure, excitement, faraway places, glamour . . .

Jet-setting is an adventure, all right—an adventure in maintaining your sanity. The only things glamorous about it are the jet setters and the destinations. Well, maybe if you're Sandra and Ricky Di Portanova, or Frank Sinatra, and you have your own plane . . .

The jumbo jet has its advantages, to be sure—lower fares and increased seating capacity have made airline travel a reality for everyone. But it has also created horrendous traffic jams, both cars and people, and turned those former good-will ambassadors, the ticket counter agents, into computor operators and cheerful, concerned hostesses into nose-to-the-grindstone workhorses with barely time to smile.

And if that isn't bad enough, making a reservation or even getting information is next to impossible. Once you're lucky enough to get through, you have to wait for fifteen minutes and listen to Muzak or some dumb recording before a reservations clerk picks up. The C.A.B. has lifted its controls, so the airlines are having a field day at trying to outdeal one another. A simple "what's the fare from Chicago to Denver?" becomes a major conversation.

Going on a trip is exciting, to be sure, but getting there certainly is a real drag. Well, travel, like hotels, can be heaven or it can be hell—it's all up to you.

First and foremost, get yourself a travel agent. Not only will it not cost you anything (they don't charge the customer but receive commissions from the airlines, hotels, shipping companies, etc.), you'll save time, money, and aggravation. They know who's got the best deals for when and where you want to go, what programs you can take advantage of for bonus miles, space-available upgrades (moves to a higher class of service than your ticket calls for) and how to get the most out of your ticket by using special routings with extra stopovers. They'll make your reservations, handle your seat selection, arrange for any special needs you have—special meals, VIP handling. They'll make your hotel reservations, arrange for limos, sightseeing, tour guides, car rentals. You name it, there is almost no aspect of your trip that you can't turn over to them.

If you're willing to make a small investment, even the airport experience can be heaven. And joining an airline club is one of the best investments a traveler can make. Traveling becomes a lot more pleasant and a lot easier when you have a friend at the airport, and private club personnel are the best "friends" you can have. If you aren't a frequent traveler, it might pay to go to the airport a few times in the guise of picking someone up and relax for a few minutes in your club, so you can start to butter the staff up, something that by this point you should be an expert at doing. You'll find that like everything else, a little extra care and planning does wonders.

You see, special accommodations are made for—and people are

upgraded—at the discretion of the agents. Those agents who seem to apply their discretion most frequently are the agents who work in the private airline clubs. Another friendly turn these agents can do is to save you money. They often exercise their authority by "overlooking" your excess baggage.

Probably the worst part of traveling is checking in, but with your new friend it will be a dream. If you let them know in advance that you're traveling, and what time to expect you to arrive at the airport, you'll be met at the ticket counter, your check-in organized, and you'll be escorted back to the club. They'll even carry your hand luggage. If you have to go right to the gate, they or a skycap they have arranged for will take you there in a cart. Of course, you can also do this yourself by simply chatting up the skycap when you give him your luggage, and augmenting your dialogue with a slightly larger tip, a big smile, and a "please."

When you board the plane, your friend will escort you on and see that you're comfortable. Impressive as hell—both to the other passengers and to the cabin crew.

In the 60s there were seven stewardesses for each 133 passengers; now there are eight cabin crew members for 450 passengers, and the services they perform have more than doubled. They aren't discourteous, they're just overworked. If you want to be "Waltzing in the Clouds," you better handle them with kid gloves; honey had better ooze from every pore. If you treat them with indifference, order them around, demand something—forget it, you're dead. You'll have to lie down in the aisle and have them trip over you before they'll bring you a cup of coffee.

Bucking for an upgrade? If you haven't accomplished it before you boarded, forget it. No story will ever be good enough. Just getting your seat changed is difficult at best.

What could be worse than to arrive in Honolulu in a mink coat and wool suit, only to discover that your luggage didn't come along? To avoid losing your luggage, don't ever check and leave it at the curb. Stay with it until you see it go down the shoot. If the skycap doesn't do it right away, tell him (smiling, of course), you aren't leaving until he does, and stand there. The same holds true if you check your luggage at the ticket counter. Watch it until it disappears from your sight. It's true you may not know where it goes from there, but at least you know it went in the direction of the baggage room in plenty of time to get on board. Believe me, this trick works. In the three years that I traveled, with thirteen pieces of luggage, I never lost one piece.

Also, be sure always to arrive at the airport at least fifty minutes to one hour before your flight—no earlier, no later. Too early and there's a good chance your luggage will go before you.

To stretch your travel dollar, take into consideration the strength of the U.S. dollar in the country to which you're traveling, if you are going to be traveling overseas. Oftentimes purchasing your international tickets abroad, including your ticket home, will cost less.

At one time, round-trip tickets were a savings, especially for foreign travel. Now, however, with standby fares and the new "all economy" airlines, the savings are questionable.

That's right. I'm suggesting economy airlines and standby— even for those who project Beverly Hills Style (with your savings, you'll be able to spend more on you). Certainly in terms of comfort and style, first-class travel takes the cake, but some of—in fact most of—the richest people I know wouldn't waste the money. I, though not rich, love comfort and find first class well worthwhile. I hate traveling any other way. Maybe that's why I'm not rich!

Need I remind you again about all the new people you'll be coming in contact with while traveling? Airline trips are no excuse for sloppy dressing, no matter how long the flight is (be sure you choose something that doesn't wrinkle easily). Besides, airlines really aren't different from restaurants and hotels: they like attractive people to dress their sets too.

Remember our traveling executive friend with the stepson? Well, just the other day she was Los Angeles bound on a flight that was overbooked in coach class and was among the twenty people who had not yet boarded. They chose her to be upgraded. When she asked, "Why me?" they replied, "Because you look so good!"

I would be remiss not to mention ships—although, aside from the QE2, they are rarely used any more to get to an actual destination except by people who refuse to fly. Ships are really a vacation in themselves.

Since every ship has its own idiosyncracies, when booking your trip be sure and ask the shipping line or travel agency for the ship's individual fact sheet. You'll find out everything you'll need to know, from tipping to dress codes, activities, and type of foods served.

If you travel on the QE2 to England, all tickets are first class, and the round trip includes a return trip on the Concorde. (If you haven't yet flown that beautiful bird, it's a real experience.)

A very elegant class of people travel the QE2, and there are almost always prominent and titled Europeans on board.

Just as in "real life," life at sea revolves around eating. Your focal point of fun, your dining room, is determined by the cost of your stateroom. If you're unhappy with the dining room to which you've been assigned, it's not essential that you upgrade your stateroom to go to a better dining room. You can go as a guest of anyone seated in any dining room, so make a few friends. Also, you can make side arrangements with the maitre d's of the individual dining rooms. Although you will be charged a small additional daily amount for the change, it will be much less than the cost of a better stateroom.

Stuck with a terrible stateroom? If you've made friends with your steward and stewardess, they just might help you out. Tip them the second you get on board and be as nice as nice can be. One gal I know, a steady ship traveler, always buys the least expensive stateroom and yet always winds up with the best. She wins the hearts of her two attendants with her southern charm, a little cash and "Oh woe is me," and winds up the winner. Just as you will, now that you know how!

ACT III
The Happy Ending: House-guesting

House-guesting, although long a European way of life, has primarily been a pastime for the fortunate few in the United States. Given the choice, the average independent American would prefer to stay in a hotel rather than impose on friends. Creatures of comfort, we prefer the easy way out. In hotels you have your independence and aren't obligated to anyone. You can come and go as you please. You can be as lazy and as messy as you want. And, you don't owe anybody anything.

The same holds true for the hostess. Although it's wonderful to have guests and to entertain them, it's a lot more wonderful when they go home. House guests can be a drain; you always have to be on your best behavior; no normal family interactions are allowed— particularly the little day-to-day squabbles. You have to give up your privacy, and you always have to be available. Having house guests is not only hard work, it means extra work. Extra cooking and extra cleaning. When you think about it, it gets expensive too; extra people to feed and to entertain. With all its disadvantages, house-guesting rarely crossed the mind of the traveling American. Or at least it didn't until recently—until the advent of the weekend-house boom. What's the fun of having a house in the country if you can't share it with your friends?

The weekend house party, a basic on the European social scene, has immigrated and, along with it, brought an end to a lot of friendships.

House-guesting is a love/hate relationship with a very strict set of rules, and if you don't abide by them it's a relationship you'll never have. You'll never be a house guest or a hostess—because no one will ever invite you again or want to come to visit you.

So, you're going to play hostess. What accommodations do you have for your guests? Do you have a comfortable room? I was once invited to stay with someone, and when I arrived I found myself sleeping on a sofa in a windowless, airless basement that had been converted into a "family room," and sharing an upstairs bathroom with her fourteen- and fifteen-year-old sons. I'm not sure if it was asphyxiation, the BVD's, the wet toilet seat (teach your sons to raise the lid, please), or the girlie pictures that got to me, but needless to say it was unpleasant, and I didn't stay very long.

As in everything else you do, you must prepare for your guests. Make their room even more comfortable—put some pretty sheets on the bed, a small, inexpensive bunch of flowers on the dresser, fresh towels and a new bar of soap in the bathroom, extra hangers in the closet, a bowl of fruit, a pitcher with ice water, and a glass on the nightstand. Have an extra blanket in the room in case it gets chilly, or, if it's hot weather, a fan.

Plan their visit, have a rough idea of what your guests like to do: i.e., antiquing, visiting historic homes, going to the theater, or just relaxing. What are the meals going to be? Are your guests the kind who help? Will you need extra help to take good care of them? Will you be dining out? If you're a late sleeper, make sure they can take care of themselves for breakfast; you won't be considered rude if you ask them to fend for themselves. If you're not sure what they drink, find out, so you'll have it. Be ready and waiting for them when they arrive; have a plate of cheese or something to nibble on. Welcome them with open arms. Let them know they're not imposing. They'll love you for making a fuss over them.

At many European house parties guests may find a typed program on their bedside table, and, along with it, a brief description or dossier on the other guests. This has not yet become the custom here, so try to discuss any set plans within the first hour or two of your guests' arrival. That way, everyone knows exactly what's expected—when the meals are, and what, if anything, to be prepared for. Always let them know the type of dress that is most appropriate for any planned activities. If you have house rules or personal idiosyncrasies, don't beat around the bush: always, always, be up-front about them.

If, God forbid, you do have some troublesome guests, depending of course on the problem, you must handle it directly. Never suffer in silence. If, for instance, the problem is simply slovenliness, I'd quite frankly avoid making an issue out of it, and just not invite them back again. On the other hand, if they're being rude and disorderly or generally making things uncomfortable for you or your other guests, I'd nip it in the bud. Unless they're really being horrible, you can't exactly ask them to leave, but you can put them on notice. Simply tell them that their behavior is unacceptable and hope they'll do something about improving it.

Next to sloppiness, the Number One hostess complaint is the guest who doesn't know when to go home. Or expects you to wait on him hand and foot while he's there. I always believe that honesty is the best policy. If someone's taking advantage, perhaps they deserve to have their feelings hurt. But, many a hostess, rather then confront the problem directly, resorts to increasingly less subtle hints. (Just please don't resort to anything as tacky as an embroidered wall placque or pillow in the guest bedroom with the message, "House guests are like fish, they both began to stink after three days." I've seen that in a number of homes I've been in, and it has made me very uncomfortable.)

One hostess I know of had a problem with a well-known international diplomat and presidential adviser who was visiting her home in the Bahamas. When the adviser and his new wife refused to acknowledge all hints to leave, the hostess manufactured an excuse to have to go back to New York and suggested they all fly together. When the foursome arrived at Kennedy, the host and hostess bid their guests adieu, breathed a sigh of relief, and boarded the next plane back to the Bahamas. Tactful but expensive!

By being aware of your guests' needs and wants, as well as your own—by keeping all of you in mind, all of the time—you'll find that everyone, including yourself, has enjoyed the visit and has had a good time.

What, you've never been a house guest? Well, you don't know what you're missing. . . .

House-guesting is not only great fun, it's also enlightening. It's often an opportunity to visit places that are somewhat off the beaten track, and although it's not free it's certainly a lot less expensive then staying in a hotel for an equal period of time. One young couple I know, Liz and John, are "professionals." Although they're poor as church mice, they've literally traveled the world and are always staying in the most fabulous places, with the most interesting people. People they've often met at another house party. They have built this way of life for themselves simply on the strength of being good guests.

THE FINE ART OF HOUSE-GUESTING, OR HOW TO BE INVITED BACK AGAIN AND AGAIN....

Be exact about the time period. Know just how long you are to stay. Try to find out what kind of visit is planned—is it dressy or casual? Take more clothes than you'll need so that you'll be ready for anything. Tell your hostess about what time to expect you, and if you're running late, even a little late, call. Don't let them worry. Always arrive with a gift in your hand and a smile on your face. The house gift doesn't have to be expensive: some wine, pâté, fine cheeses, homemade cookies, or a knick-knack.

This is no time for moodiness or introspection. If ever there's a time when you should plan on being charming, disarming, and witty, it's while you're house-guesting. Smile, laugh, be on!

If your hostess is someone you know and love, it's easy to arrive with hugs and kisses; if it's a first visit, walk in with open eyes and compliments on your lips. It's a time to be grateful in advance for all the kindnesses that are going to be shown to you from start to finish. Always remember, you're in someone else's house and your host and hostess have their own rules, their own way of doing things. You can't continue to live exactly as you do at home. So go with the flow! Actually, that's a big part of the fun of going away—to experience new lifestyles, new people, new foods, new things.

It doesn't take much effort to figure out how much work goes into taking care of house guests, so be a good one. Keep your room neat, the bed made, the towels hung up, and *never* leave smoldering cigarettes in the ashtray. Be helpful in the kitchen. If you're a good cook, offer to prepare one of the meals, including buying the ingredients; if you're a kitchen klutz, or your offer is rejected, why not take your hosts out for a meal or do something else you're good at—set tables, do the flower arrangements, do some shopping, fix drinks for everyone. Entertain the hostess while she's fixing dinner. You know, tell stories, or read something amusing aloud. If there is no household help, do more than your share of cleaning. If you're house-guesting in Europe, they'll have help and you'll be expected to give the help a small tip when you leave (not a bad idea in the U.S. either). If you're an early riser and your hostess isn't, get coffee-making instructions. In Europe, they'll ask you when you'd like your tray, and your breakfast will be served in your room.

As you might expect, some of the no-no's of life also hold true when house-guesting. Obviously you will *not* drink too much; you will *not* make a fool of yourself by flirting with anyone you shouldn't be flirting with; you will *not* argue with your hosts or any of their guests; and you'll always remember whose house it is. When you return home, write a loving note, mentioning all the wonderful things your hosts did to make you feel so comfortable.

House-guesting—what better way is there to spend a few days than in the bosom of friends? And what a joy it is to know that they'll want to embrace you over and over again!

12

On the Road

The rock star has his limo, the good ole boy (outside of Texas, that is) his pickup, the surfer his Woody, the working gal her Japanese compact with it's cutesy name, the college professor his Peugeot 504, the environmental activist his Honda Civic, the Ivy Leaguer his Volvo or Saab, and the Aspen and Vale Snow Bunnies their Range Rover or their Willys. Even our Synonymees have their "group identifier" or image perpetuator.

What else would a Beverly Hills Swinger (BHS) drive other than something that shouts a carefree love of life—something fast, foreign, and sexy. Our Brooks Brothers Billboard (BBB's) are lovers of the Euro Turbo or maybe, just maybe, a Mercedes Diesel.

As urban dwellers, our Upwardly Mobile Maven (UMM) is traditionally not a car owner, but if he does indulge, it's a difficult decision. Oddly enough he's torn between going BBB with the Euro Turbo, or swinging along Beverly Hills Style. His route of action will depend upon whether that family portrait (see page 120) is real or fake. If it's fake, he's chugging along in his Saab.

If ever there was a perfect match, it's the International Jet Setter (IJSer) and an Italian sports car. Quite accustomed to genteel poverty, the IJSer doesn't really care if the car is expensive, only that its noisy. A bit more accustomed to using OPM (Other People's Money) than his own, he is perfectly content to enjoy OPC's (Other People's Cars), whatever make they happen to be. That's as long as it's not a beige or powder-blue four-door sedan. To the MOR, Detroit is Big Daddy. For New York Chic, it's a long black limo or an older sedan with a driver. And since it had better be elegant to belong to a Tasteful and Accessorized (T&A), what else could it be but a Bentley, generally a bit on in years.

And the Terrific, Trendy, and Deadly (TTDer) likes his cars the way he likes his clothes—whatever it is, you won't expect it. They are the most individualistic: hot rods, '58 Caddie convertibles, a 1966 Bronze Buick Wildcat.

CARS—STATUS SYMBOLS OR IMAGE PERPETUATERS?

Just ask Don Rickles what his favorite thing is:

> My Rolls Royce. From childhood on I dreamed of owning one because it represented the peak of achievement and success. Now that I have one, it always (almost always) stays in my garage. It's cared for like a baby, constantly washed and polished. I get upset if even a speck of dust falls on it.

"If you've got it, flaunt it" is the Beverly Hiller's byline. Cut off from their ties that bind, where nobody knows from whence they came (but rarely was it from old money), they believe in telling you who they are and where they're at. Their chief vehicle of expression is their second home—their car.

Although Beverly Hills itself is only 5.69 square miles, the square mileage of Los Angeles county is 4,083, and the average Beverly Hiller might drive several hundred miles a day and spend hours in the car. Nothing is just down the block or around the corner. Everything is sixteen dry cleaners and a Taco Bell away. You'd be hard-pressed to say to anyone, "see you in fifteen minutes"—the only thing that's fifteen minutes away is your tennis court!

Beverly Hills. Where the *minimum* building requirement standard is a three-car garage, and the average is five—with cars to fill every slot. And every Beverly Hills family is either a one-Mercedes, a one-Jaguar, or a one-something-exotic family.

Beverly Hillers have often been accused of being in love with their cars. When one has air-conditioned garages, does this mean love? In Beverly Hills there is no greater star! It's not that we're attached to our cars; it's just that to us, they aren't "just cars." You'll never hear a Beverly Hiller refer to his car simply as his "car." It's always "My 450 is getting a tuneup," or "My Jag is acting up."

But in Beverly Hills are cars really status symbols? Well, maybe for the movie studio head a Rolls is a status symbol. But what difference does it make if it's only leased or it's part of his "deal." If someone else is paying the tab, that makes him *real important.*

But does Rod Stewart need a status symbol? What else would he drive but his Lamberghini?

Could Dino Martin have pulled up in front of Beverly Hills High in anything other than a new Ferrari?

And doesn't Michael Caine belong in his Rolls?

And Jacqueline Bisset and Heather Thomas in their Jaguars?

And let's face it. Sidney Sheldon has been on the bestseller list so many times he doesn't drive a Rolls to prove a point.

And everyone knows that Robert Wagner, Robert Stack, and Ozzie Smith are important actors. I don't think they drive Mercedes to prove it. And neither does Merv Griffin.

Look at how long Ann-Margret's been a star. Wouldn't you be surprised to see her in anything but her Rolls Royce?

And I don't think a Dodge Dart is exactly Superman's style, but his Mercedes certainly is.

And although the heaviest thing they ever carry is a wallet, isn't a pickup just what you'd expect Clint Eastwood and James Garner to drive? Certainly a far cry from a status symbol.

Could you imagine Liberace driving anything other than a custom Caddy with piano keyboard upholstery and a candelabra hood ornament?

And when you think about it, isn't Kathy Lee Crosby more at home behind the wheel of her Corvette, and Victoria Principal behind the wheel of her Porsche, than they would be behind the wheel of a Chevy?

Sometimes what we assume someone's image to be isn't. Take the Texan, for instance. You probably imagine that Texans drive Cadillacs and pickups. Wrong on both counts. That's Midwest and Oklahoma Plain. Them good ole Texas boys have tucked away their cowboy boots and BBQ, their Caddies and pickups. Sure, they're still truckin', but it ain't in any pickup, 'cause they just don't look good parked at them chic cafés and French gourmet restaurants. Now it's slick Eyetalian jackets and Ferraris, Masseratis, Jaguars, and Mercedes. What's happened? According to Steve Forrestal of Forrestal GT Cars in Houston, "We're go-getters, expressing ourselves. Texans are movers, we live in the fast lane."

If you were back East, it would be a different story. To the Westchesterite, the Backbay Bostonian, or Philadelphia Main Liner, Mercedes means "nouveau." They'd prefer to make their understatement with the Euro Turbo: the Audi, BMW, Peugeot, or the Notchback Saab—the boxier the better. What does this say about their personality?

New Yorkers are far too sophisticated for images and symbols, and cars are *not* one of their priorities. Unless, of course, the car is outfitted with the necessities . . . a ticker tape, a manicurist, a shoeshine boy, and a hotline to his girlfriend and his wife, with prerecorded messages: "I'm on the way, baby. . . ." "Sorry, dear, I'm stuck in a meeting. . . ." Oh, and it's got to be long and black. And as far as *she's* concerned, as long as it's there waiting for her outside Bergdorf Goodman's and there is someone to carry her packages. . . . Meanwhile, back on the streets, fantasies are being fulfilled at least twelve times a day. The car of *their* dreams is yellow, has a light on the top, and its off-duty sign isn't lit.

In the Midwest, where Detroit is in the driver's seat, your symbol used to be determined not only by your financial and professional status but also by your marital status. Once the ring was on the finger, it was the memory of single days of Corvettes, Firebirds, and Camaros that helped propel the Oldsmobile Cutlass down the Kennedy Expressway to the Loop. But alas and alack, even the Big Four are having trouble holding back the German invasion in those midwestern cities, and now you can't tell the single men from the married men because they're all driving BMW's, Porsches, and Mercedes diesels.

Southern Gentlemen and their little ladies like their cars just as they like their life—*real easy.* You know, big, soft, and comfortable; a kind of plantation on wheels. Lincolns and Cadillacs are their mint juleps. And where do these luxury liners go to retire? To Florida, where else?

THE ULTIMATE FANTASY

If Mr. Anthony knocked on your door and said, "John Beresford Tipton wants you to have the car of your dreams," what would you get?

The car, a technical invention with an impact that surpassed all others, is more than just a means of transportation. Indeed, it's had an overwhelming effect in changing the landscape of our cities and our lifestyles. It represents you. The you you are, or the you you'd like to become. Just sit behind the wheel of your fantasy car and see what happens. Watch the change come over you and know that's just how you were meant to feel, and its just where you belong. And some day before you know it, it's right where you're going to be.

13

Home Chic Home

Are you a "Stranger in a Strange Land"; do you ever wake up in the morning and wonder where you are? Do you ever feel like an alien in an alien environment? Is your castle a prison, a contrived creation that reflects an expression of someone else? Is your home composed of bits and pieces, frustrating afterthoughts that traumatize the spirit? Do you ever feel nervous and ill at ease for no apparent reason? Have you ever really *thought* about your home and the effect it actually has on *you?*

Your home. It should be your sanctuary—your security blanket, providing you with warmth and safety, the place where you can find inner peace and happiness.

Your home. It's the strongest personal statement you can make. It doesn't have to be a picture from a magazine or a decorator's dream or a furniture store advertisement or a period piece. It just has to be *you*. Like your clothes, it's an expression of you; your needs, your lifestyle, your interests, and your involvements. Where you go, what you do, what you like!

Do you remember how you felt in Chapter Five, Act II, All Dressed Up and Someplace to Go, when you went shopping and tried on the Synonymee Image Outfits? Forget for a minute how they looked. I'm talking about how they felt—or perhaps I should say, how they made you feel. There must have been some that you couldn't wait to take off, that made you feel nervous or foolish. Why? Not because they looked terrible but because they weren't you. Because they weren't an expression of you—the you you are or the you you wanted to become. Your house or apartment could be having the same effect on you.

It might have been love at first sight, but before you decided to move in you gave it some thought. You had to be certain that it would be comfortable and functional.

Decision made, you began to decorate. Perhaps you started looking through home furnishing magazines, browsed in stores, studied what your friends had done, or hired an interior decorator. Or maybe your new home wiped you out financially and you didn't have many choices.

You might have thought: what difference does it make, it's only furniture, and if it looks okay... So you just made do with what you or someone else had. Tell me, how do you feel when you put on just any old thing, or you're wearing someone else's clothes? How many castoffs and hand-me-downs do you have in your closet?

Perhaps you decided to really go the route and "furnish." How many pieces of furniture got as much thought as the dress you're wearing? How many of them did you "try on"? Did you buy things that you saw in magazines, because you liked the way they looked? Do you buy your clothes from a catalogue? If you saw an ensemble in a magazine, or a newspaper, would you buy it simply because you liked the way it looked, or would you try it on first? If you did decide to buy it, on what would you base your decision? It looked good, and felt good—it was flattering and comfortable; you felt relaxed in it. It was practical—it served a purpose, it allowed you to carry on the functions of your life. Most important, it said something about YOU—it reflected your lifestyle. Look around you. Is your house or apartment doing all that? Because it should be.

Have you created a set, fit for a star, that's letting your glow shine through? Is it YOUR STAGE? Are you surrounded by your props? Is it for your enjoyment?

If you read a lot, why don't you have a comfortable spot—a good reading chair and a lamp? Why do you have a big public area if you don't entertain? If you don't give dinner parties, why on earth do you have an elaborate dining room? Please tell me, why invest money in a showplace if nobody's going to see it? If you're a compulsive workaholic, if you go to work early and come home late, if you're hardly ever home, perhaps all you need is a comfortable nest—a port in the storm, a refuge from the madness. If you're the kind who likes to come home, get into a robe, and tuck into bed with your dinner on a tray and watch T.V., why haven't you done more with your bedroom?

And speaking of bedrooms, how's your bed? What kind of mattress do you like, hard or soft? What kind do you have? And you wonder why you're so irritable! By the way, do you have a set of "special" sheets for that "special" company, or for when you just want to indulge *you*? If you're not good to you, how can you expect anyone else to be?

Oh, you do entertain a lot; you're "the hostess with the mostest," mostest friends, mostest stories to tell, mostest laughs to share. Is your house arranged to suit that style? Do you have a good circle of furniture in a conversational grouping, maybe around a big low coffee table which can double as a dining room table with cushions on the floor for informal occasions?

What kind of person are you? Are you what you'd call traditional, softly feminine; or "a man's man," the home-spun and Sunday-dinner type? Then why are you surrounded by stark colors, sharp lines, modern art, and hi-tech? No wonder you're so uptight. Aren't round arms and squashy pillows a bit easier to "wear?" Aren't those stark white walls shocking to your system? Wouldn't a warm peach be somewhat more of a caress?

If you're really lighthearted and frivolous, perhaps it's all that heavy dark wood and leather furniture that your mother brought with her when she came from Germany that's depressing you. Maybe that's what's making you so "heavy."

For reasons unknown to you, everyone has always thought of you as solid and sedate, when you're really a fireball—avant-garde and very SEXY? Well, those beige blah walls and that beige blah carpeting won't bring that out in you, but deep red walls with a zebra rug will.

But, you know, you're not the only one whose surroundings are a bit of a contradiction. Many stars, people whom you would think really know themselves, who seem so "in touch," project something completely different from the way they live. For instance, it would have never occurred to me that Woody Allen would sleep in a blue and white, four-poster canopy bed with a rocking chair next to it.

Or that Cher, with her butterfly-tattooed bottom, would ever have lived in a Tuscan-style estate with *very* formal period rooms containing graceful French pieces, gentle colors and textures—and sleeping in, of all things, an exquisitely carved four-poster renaissance bed.

Somehow, I would never expect Buddy Hacketts' study to be a fortress of rifles.

Or Barbara Walters to be the black, white, and red type who would furnish her living room with what was originally a "summer solution for sofas scheduled to be reupholstered." Bold black and white vine-patterned slipcovers and a group of throw pillows—all in different contrasting designs, on top of an Iranian throw rug?

Somehow, when I listen to the gentle strains of Joni Mitchell singing "California," it's beyond my comprehension that her bedroom is a reflection of her; yet it's her favorite room—a draped bronze four-poster bed in an elevated alcove, with an extremely bold-patterned carpet.

It sure beats me. I would think that if anyone knew who they were and how to express it in their surroundings, it would be the stars.

According to my good friend Phyllis Morris, internationally renowned consultant to decorators and an authority on people and furniture—she's worked with more stars than Hitchcock—"Not necessarily. In fact, quite the contrary. Stars are professional performers, and the thing they know best is what they do. The other thing they're very knowledgable about is that in other areas, particularly in furnishing and creating environments, they need guidance."

She went on to confirm what we've already become so aware of, how often what the stars project professionally is really quite a different image from what they *really* are. "Take the sex symbols, the ones you'd expect to have the sensuous bedrooms." (Phyllis is famed for designing mirrored and upholstered beds.) "Are you kidding? Most of them wouldn't put the lights on if their lives depended on it. They could never sleep in one of my mirror-backed canopy beds. They're often so unsure of their bodies they would freak out if they had to look at themselves while they were in bed."

"But how do you know what makes people tick?" I asked.

"I go right upstairs and look in their closets." Understandable, when you think what clothes tell about a person. But that wasn't all she had in mind. "Bedrooms tell a lot about a person. People frequently project one image in their public rooms, but their private rooms are quite another story." She told me about one man, someone we all know and love who, despite his very straight downstairs rooms and image, had quite an opposite type of bedroom: black leather, whips and chains. Also, and quite common among show people (that's "show" as in "show and tell"), there are the ones who never invite you to see the upstairs. The ones who can't afford what isn't on view.

We laughed about one Beverly Hills gal, veeery impressed with herself and her megabucks—at least, that's what it seemed like from external appearances. Not only did she own and live on a magnificent estate; in addition, she had purchased what is probably the most impressive and famous estate in Beverly Hills, high in Trousdale Estates. The big joke was that when someone left the elaborately furnished downstairs to take a peek at the bedrooms, she discovered that the entire second floor, except for mattresses, was empty.

Phyllis went on, "A good designer has to be part psychiatrist and use a lot of ESP." She reminded me of an assignment she had taken on for me a few years ago and my own Phyllis Morris Room. I know it's difficult to imagine, looking at me now (ha-ha), but sexiness hasn't always been one of my strong suits, so I asked Phyllis to create my ultimate "love nest." It was not what one would typically imagine a love nest to be—all Oriental—but it brought out my best. Eventually, it had to double as a waiting room, and I wasn't the only one affected by its sex magic. I'd often go to collect my diet clients who were waiting for their appointments with me and find them locked in an embrace. (Linda Ronstadt and Governor Jerry Brown, among them.)

I asked Phyllis about the problems people have with many designers; the designers who impose their fantasies on the client at the clients' expense instead of artistically expressing their clients' needs. She explained that she rarely works with clients directly but is instead a consultant to other interior designers. These designers bring clients from all over the world to her Beverly Hills showroom, not only to buy her furniture but also for her expertise in zeroing in on and expressing the personality of the client. The first thing she does with them is send them into the "fitting room."

There is no other way to describe Phyllis's multimillion dollar showroom, which has forty different environments. Try, if you will, to imagine the most exciting page from *Architectural Digest*. Multiply that vision tenfold, put it into real life, and you'll have a conservative description of Phyllis's world. From Country Kitchen to Traditional, Oriental, white satin and marble, mirrors, lacquered California Glitz.

How do people react when they're asked to see "which shoe fits?" Well, Keith Moon of The Who didn't want to take any chances on selecting his bedroom, so he and his girlfriend sampled a few beds. Without clothing—how else?

"But what if a person has several moods, or doesn't want to make a long-term commitment to 'a look?' Can you change furniture like you do clothing?" I asked, trying to twist the little tags so I could see some prices. It could be a mighty expensive hobby, I discovered. The lowest-priced room in the showroom runs about $40,000, and they go up into the $80's. Furniture isn't cheap, even when it's a room that supposedly is done at a bargain rate. Phyllis pointed out that the average room you might see in a *Women's Day* magazine costs about $20,000.

For the person with multiple dwellings, the trend is to do different looks. Different spaces and multifaceted personalities require different styles. The new apartment that Phyllis just did for Dick Clark in the Trump Tower in Manhattan is a total departure from his California beach house. For New York, he has an exotic bedroom with a wall-to-wall-ceiling-to-floor-corniced Deco-styled-dusty-rose-lacquered bed. In California, it's a very traditional beach look.

Phyllis pointed out, however, that one wouldn't necessarily buy "a room" in toto but would often mix and match. Sarah Purcell's new house is a good example. Although it basically has a sophisticated country motif, there are touches of the Far East, which include some very important Oriental pieces.

Nothing seems to be a challenge for this gal who wears so many hats, except perhaps wearing the hats (she hates getting her hair messed up and has to have it done daily). A mere twenty-five years ago Phyllis first established herself as a Beverly Hills designer; now she has showrooms all over the world. She's been a regular on "A.M. Los Angeles," is a celebrated party giver (see Parties With Pizazz chapter); has a newspaper column, which is internationally syndicated in over two hundred newspapers, and has written an exposé, *Behind the Guarded Gates*, destined to be a best seller. Add to that list of credits, a furniture-movie-set designer. Gone are the days of the backless desks and sofas. Realistic acting requires realistic props—and believe me, modern-day movie makers spare no expense, either in talent or in props. That gorgeous lacquered desk that Joan Collins sits at in "Dynasty" is a Phyllis Morris design; a mere trifle at $12,000.

"Surely you've had one challenge," I pleaded.

"Welllllll . . ." she hesitated for a moment, thinking. She came up with one—her good friend, the writer Harold Robbins—but was quick to add that the challenge was "only for a second." The one thing he needed for his study in his new Beverly Hills home: no distractions. He needed to be able to focus all his attention on the page in his typewriter. He got just what he asked for. Believe me, he sees the white page of that paper, and that's it. It might read hot, scorching red, but all he's seeing is white—bright, hot, white against a black backdrop. And when I say black, I mean BLACK. Black walls, black desk, black chair, black leather roman blinds; even a black no-light, no-ring telephone. The only distraction— mounted in a separate metal frame—is the first page of each of his novels. Another of Phyllis' novel ideas!

But how does all this help you? If you can't afford to completely redo but want to live in Beverly Hills Style, where do you begin? Well, there are many not-so-expensive ways to make your home a "Mr. Blandings' Dream House." It's going to require time and, you'll pardon the pun, homework (reading lots of decorating magazines)—and, like everything else you do, planning!

I asked my favorite decorator (and, I'm proud to say, one of Chicago's and La Jolla, California's foremost interior designers) what she thinks. Now you might say I'm a bit prejudiced, but I also have good taste. Good enough taste to have been born into the right family. One of our team of experts is my mother, Esther Mazel. Her first suggestion: "Start shopping. Find out what you want, look through all the magazines, go to furniture stores. If you live in a city where there is a furniture mart, go there and browse. Since they are for wholesale buyers, you won't be able to buy anything or go into most of the showrooms, but you can see what they've got through their windows."

In actual fact, I happen to know that many of the showrooms will let you in, particularly at the Merchandise Mart in Chicago. Although you still can't buy, you can look. George Johnson, the vice president of Knoll Furniture, whose showroom is strictly for the trade, told me about a man who used to come to his showroom every day and sit for an hour. No one knew him, and when they asked what he was doing and why he was there, he replied, "It makes me feel good." They got a kick out of him and looked forward to his daily visits.

Another of Esther's suggestions is model homes. "They are a terrific way of looking at furniture. The more expensive the home, obviously the better it is going to be furnished. Department stores, many of which have extensive furniture departments, are another good place for getting ideas. If you see something you like, something you think suits you, feel it out. Sit in it, and among it, and try to stay as long as you can—as long as they'll let you. Don't buy anything until you really give it some forethought. Remember, furniture isn't clothing, you're not going to cast it aside next season. It's not a car, you're not going to turn it in, in a few years. It's a major investment, so don't just rush out blind."

If it's within your budget, Esther strongly recommends hiring an interior decorator. Oftentimes, although they charge a fee and/or commission on what you buy, you'll save money in the long run. "Many times people don't need as much as they think. Many things can be salvaged with just a few new additions, or a change in floor coverings or window treatments." (Barbara Walters certainly isn't above using slipcovers!)

"How do you find the right interior designer for you?" I asked. "You hear so many horror stories, and decorators have been the brunt of so many jokes."

It seems most of Esther's clients have come by way of referral, so asking "Who did it?" if you're in someone's home you like is usually a good bet. If you go to model homes, the name of the designer is always displayed, and home furnishing stories in newspapers always include the designers' names. Magazines, society or gossip columns often mention things about the "in" decorator of the day. However, going with Mr. Big just because he's Mr. Big isn't always the best choice because that's where you'll usually find the big egos that overwhelm a client with their ideas. The interior designer trade association, A.S.I.D. (American Society of Interior Designers), will also give you referrals.

You'll know if the designer is right for you by having an introductory meeting, not a consultation but simply a meeting for each of you to check the other out. Esther pointed out that the client is also on trial. "Nobody wants a 'headache,' a client who insists on something that is downright awful. After all, the designer's work is his showcase, his calling card. We have reputations to maintain. Always remember, the designers are the professionals, so be prepared to listen and to take their advice.

"In this initial meeting try to get a feel not only for the designer, to see if you have rapport, but also try to see what she would do—how she views you. Obviously, she isn't going to give away all her trade secrets, but you should be able to tell if you're simpatico."

What if you can't afford a decorator, or you can't pay cash for your furniture (a story I've known well)—then what do you do? Esther's recommendation was just what we did when we furnished what became the birthplace of the Beverly Hills Diet Center: charge it at major department stores and furniture stores and get guidance from their in-house person. (I didn't have to do that, of course—I had Esther!) If, however, you're going to be shopping at several places, get input only from one store decorator or you'll get confused and wind up with a mishmash of ideas.

"What do you do," I asked, "when you have a client who wants something that seems absolutely wrong?"

"If you're a good decorator, it's usually not a problem. You have to give people what they want. The key is guiding them, so whatever they want is in good taste." She told me a story about a woman who wanted a look that was the exact antithesis of *her*. She was about 5'5", dark, fiery, a real cute personality, but she weighed over two hundred pounds. Esther would have selected earth tones and big, casual, floppy furniture. The client, on the other hand, wanted blues and mauves and a softly feminine look. The end result was a two-chaise living-room arrangement, and though not at all like her, it was elegantly styled, in good taste—and it made the client very happy. In fact, she remarked that it made her feel like "Dynasty's" Alexis.

"But then what happened?" I asked. "After she had to live with it for a while, didn't she feel out of place? Didn't it make her feel uncomfortable?"

Smiling, Esther replied, "What happened to her should happen to everybody who would like to better themselves, who lives in a fantasy world of who they would like to be. I didn't hear from her for about four months, then one evening the telephone rang. It was my client, calling back to thank me. It seems she had lost forty pounds and had given up her job working in her parents' store and had gone back to school."

Look around you. Are your surroundings shouting YOU? Are they worthy of YOU? Frank Lloyd Wright once said, "A man lives up to his surroundings." Perhaps it's now time you created one that YOU'D LIKE TO BE WORTHY OF!

14

Welcome to Paradise

Welcome to The Garden of Eden—Beverly Hills. You've done it, now you're here. Welcome to Paradise. Welcome to a world of new beginnings, dreams come true, and living happily ever after. You have entered a rarified world; and it really doesn't matter if you live in Des Moines, Iowa, Detroit, Michigan, or Raleigh, North Carolina. Beverly Hills isn't a place, it's a fantasy. It's a state of being that exists in our imagination. It's a world of images, success, and fulfilled potential. Congratulations, you've made it. Now, you too can have anything you want, because now you know that you can get it; you know how to go after it. Now that you believe in yourself.

Gone are the days of would've, should've, if only, and but. Instead it's I will, I can, I want to. You've eliminated the one obstacle in your life—*you*. Now there is nothing blocking your path to success. You've broken the debilitating self-inhibiting cycle once and for all—and forever. You've erased the tape and replaced it with a pride and self-confidence you never knew you possessed. You've taken control of the essence of your life and put it to work for you. You've learned how to exploit the synergy of your mind and your heart. You've turned on your GO POWER, and your DFC is operating full speed ahead. You're all-powerful, a joyful testimony to your success.

In the months that you've spent rehearsing my scripts, you've learned that the Beverly Hills Style is nothing more than a technique, a technique that you can easily acquire and integrate into your life. By understanding, accepting, and conceptualizing the concept I CAN you've unleashed your wildest fantasies. They have now become as much a reality in your consciousness as any of your mundane daily chores. And as one by one you've seen these fantasies become reality, you've seen how automatic it all just becomes.

And now that your support system is secure, you don't need anyone else. You've learned not to depend on anybody but YOU. You've turned your life around, and you're coming out on top.

And with each day that passes, as your strength of self grows and gains momentum, you find you are making fewer and fewer excuses. As you hear yourself initiate conversations, even sparkle in them, as one by one you turn those formerly embarrassing I could-have-died situations to your advantage, as you walk into a room and you see heads turn and you hear the hush, you realize that you have no reason to be anything but vital, alive, and full of hope.

But you're not a fool, you know that not every problem in your life has been eliminated; it's not that all of your liabilities are gone, but the Beverly Hills Style has helped you eliminate the biggest, your negative energy. Your lack of belief in you! Until now, your negativity encompassed your life and tainted your world. You were coming from a core of imperfection. Now it's your belief in you, your positive energy, that nourishes you and has freed you for living. And now, at long last, you're experiencing life happening your way. You're making it happen your way.

The people who were the downers, who perpetuated "impossible" and "no, you can't," have been eliminated from your life. Your world is alive with other believers, people who speak your language and share your enthusiasm. They reinforce your belief in YOU.

Beware, though—negativity is still as near as tomorrow, and will stop at nothing to reclaim you. It lies poised like a snake—coiled, ready to strike. When you hear its voice, preying on your vulnerability, saying "I can't, it's too hard, it won't work," know that it exists but don't listen to it, and don't dwell on it. Now that you've grasped the core of this good life and all it has to offer, embrace it and hold on tight. Don't ever give in, and don't ever give up. Instead, rejoice in YOU; in your accomplishments. Enjoy YOU, and appreciate YOU. You deserve it; you've earned it. The Beverly Hills Style has become a part of you, and it becomes you. The YOU you always hoped and knew you could be.

You've become part of a very special world, a world belonging to those who seek and effect the impossible, who dare to "dream the impossible dream." Your success is the living testimony to the wonders of The Beverly Hills Style. Shout your victory to the world and let me welcome you into "our world," into the world of believers, with your own badge of courage—the gold palm tree pin, the symbol of The Beverly Hills Styler. Our badge of success!

Send me a copy of your records from your workbook, and I'll send you your Beverly Hills Style Certificate of Achievement and your little golden palm tree pin along with information on The Beverly Hills Style world and ways to plug in. (See page 263 for address.)

If you ever need me, if you have any questions, I'm only as far away as your pen. I'm not worried about you, though; I know you'll do just fine. Well, why wouldn't you? You've already proved that anything is possible—if you just let yourself dream.

A bridge isn't built before it's someone's idea
A skyscraper can't be erected before someone designs it
Everything in life begins with an idea
Reality
It's nothing more then fantasy realized
A dream is a wish to build a world upon, and no star is too far away
Dream, and you shall have.

Style [and, I might add, the Beverly Hills Style] is being yourself on purpose. . . . Now you must know precisely who you are, but you need the confidence to show it. And because you have style means you go out on a limb. . . . To be sure, having style takes a fair degree of confidence and a certain amount of chutzpah!

—Raquel Welch

Thank you, Raquel, for summing it all up for me.

Judy Mazel

Appendix 1

Now that you know how to play the game, it's time to do so. Although some of you will prefer to keep your stage in "your own backyard," there will be many of you who will prefer to venture out into the world; to spread your wings. In either case, have fun—don't be afraid, and always remember: no matter who you are or where you've come from, the whole world is your stage and everyone in it your co-stars. Including THE STYLE SETTERS.

THE STYLE SETTERS

The STARS of the screen, stage, and *social world*—the people who set the trends. They move in their own special world—a world we read about in Jody's column, Suzy's column, and Maxine's column. It's a world that they own, that they have created. It's a world in which they are catered to because it's a world that is dependent upon them for its very existence. It's a world, P.S., that *anyone* can buy his or her way into.

THE CHIC SEEN is the who, what, where, and when of THE STYLE SETTERS.

Unfortunately space permits only the highlights of this Ultra World. Every city has its social watering holes, hotels, as well as its who's who, debutante balls, galas, social and cultural events, private clubs, private schools, places to shop, special hairdressers, right manicurists, "in" doctors, and preferred addresses. And then, of course, there are the shoots and hunts, horse shows, fishing spots, spas, hideaways . . . You'll find it all in Le Chic Seen Comprehensive Roster (page 263).

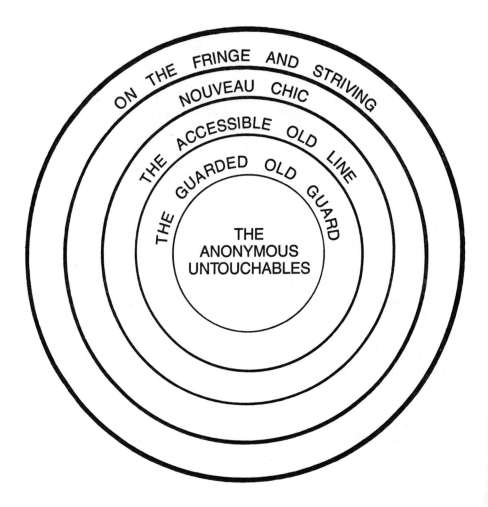

Cafe Society and Nescafe Society, the Who's Who and Where of the Inner Circle of the Social Scene

Far be it from me to cast aspersions, to classify anyone. I'll leave that to you. You see, I don't want to lose my prize table at Ma Maison or Le Cirque, and I hate waiting at the bar at the Bistro Garden, all of which are signs that you've been ostracized from THE CHIC SEEN. So I'll let you match the names with their ranking. If there are some names, and there probably are, that you don't recognize, do a little homework. If you're going to move with the "movers and shakers," you have to kinow who they are. I will give you one hint, however: the two innermost circles are accessible only by birth or through marriage.

You will note that the stars of the entertainment world have been omitted from the following list because they're in a world all their own. Besides, you know who THEY are.

The Baron and Baroness Di Portanova
  (Sandra and Ricky)
Gordon and Ann Getty
Alfred and Judy Taubman
Philip and Suzy Gutfriend
Donald and Yvonna Trump
Sid and Ann Bass
Jimmy and Charlene Niederlander
Doris Duke
Bill and Simone Levitt
Sonny and MaryLou Whitney
Lee Radziwill
Jackie Onassis
Nan Kempner
Dr. Aldo Gucci
The DeYoung Family
John and Patricia Kluge
Jack and Ethel Hausman
Austine Hearst
Norton and Jennifer Simon

Amanda Burden
Tom Burden
Bunker and Caroline Hunt
Toddye Lee Wynne
Jan Barboglio MacDonald
Trudy Glossberg
Barbara Grimes
Kathy Perlmutter
John and Bonnie Swearingen
Lady Sarah Armstrong Jones
. H. Ross Perot
Oscar and Lynn Wyatt
Joanne Herring
Laura Hunt
C. Z. Guest
Joan Schnitzer
Brooke Astor
Donina Cicogna
Arianna Stassinopoulos
Ahmet Mica Ertegun

Cubby and Dana Brocolli
Jerry Zipkin
Harry and Leona Helmsley
Mowin Davis
Barbara DePortago
Louis and P.A.B. Widener III
Rhea and Ann Chamness
Jacque Wynne
Bradley and Twinkle Bayoud
Ruth Sharp
Francis Lowell Coolidge
Charles Duell

Bill and Pat Buckley
Permelia Reed
Henry and Jane Berger
Larry and Marcia Israel
Kay Auchincloss
Jayne Wrightsman
Sherwood and Judy Weisner
Brenda Johnson
Arlene Walsh
Laura Charlton
Sarah Fullwinder
Heather Callahan

WHERE THE CHIC MEET

Where the Chic Meet is a month by month calendar of the "in" vacation spots around the world. The where and when of the social scene of The Style Setters.

There are several places mentioned that by some standards are considered relics of the past. Au contraire, The Style Setters have just tucked themselves away in their not-so-little villas and are simply not as visible as they have been in the past. These spots will be denoted by an *. If you don't know where these places are, once again, do your homework.

January
Gstaad
St. Moritz
Barreloche
Cortina
Deer Park
St. Barts
Lyford Cay
Palm Beach

February
Rio de Janiero
Mistique
St. Barts
Venice (film crowd)
Punta del Este
Palm Beach
Deer Park
Gstaad

March
Mistique
Beverly Hills (Academy Awards)
Morocco (Easter)
Hawaii (West Coast crowd)
Palm Springs (West Coast crowd)

April
Paris
New York
Cannes (Film crowd)
Palm Springs

May
(Not a great traveling month. Everyone
 is home, recuperating and losing
 weight from the winter to get ready
 for the summer.)
Palm Springs

June
London
Mikonos
Marmaris

July
Monte Carlo
St. Tropez
Positano
Portillo
Capri* (if Valentino has a villa there,
   it is hardly passé.)
Kahala Hilton (West Coast crowd)
Marbella* (playground of the
   Middle Eastern chic shiek)
Hamptons
Newport

August
(See July)
Saratoga
Deauville

September
South of France (all over)
Montecatini

October
New York
London
Paris
Scotland, France, Spain
   (bird and boar shoots)

November
Shoot areas (See Oct.)
New York
London

December
Leche
St. Barts
Egypt
Barreloche
Deer Park

WHERE THE CHIC SLEEP

A sampling of hotels around the world where you are certain to see important people.

The Beverly Hills Hotel, Beverly Hills
L'Ermitage, Beverly Hills
The Mayfair Regent, New York
The Regency, New York
The Pierre, New York
The Ritz Carlton, Boston
The Mansion on Turtle Creek, Dallas
Palm Bay, Miami
Claridge's, London
Qisisanna, Capri
El Hassler Villa Medici, Rome
Marbella Club, Marbella
Hôtel Du Cap, Cap d' Antibes
San Pietro, Positano
Cipriani, Venice
Peninsula, Hong Kong (perhaps not as gorgeous and modern as the
     Regent, but definitely chicer and more elegant)
Oriental, Bangkok
Giraffe Manor, Kenya
Mala Mala, South Africa
Ritz, Paris
Bristol, Paris
Kahala Hilton, Honolulu
Copacabana Palace (In desperate need of modernization and repair
     and certainly there are a number of hotels in Rio that are newer,
     "prettier," and much more modern, but they don't hold a candle
     to the Copacabana Palace when it comes to the crowd.)

WHERE THE CHIC GET BEAT

The sporting life is very much a part of the way of life of The Style Setter, however as in everything else, they are very particular about how and where they will lose their money and expend their "rooting for" energy.

Casinos
Monte Carlo
Baden-Baden
Divonne le Bain

Horse Racing
The Kentucky Derby (The row to
 watch—L—Millionaires Row)
Pimlico
Belmont
Saratoga
Deaville
Arc de Triomphe
Royal Ascot (You must be in The
 Royal Enclosure)
Goodwood

Polo
Summer
Westbury (Invitational Cup)
Saratoga
Meadowbrook
Santa Barbara
England, France, Germany

Winter
Palm Beach (Piaget World Cup)
Palm Springs
Argentina

Croquet
Winter
International Tournament,
Palm Beach
Summer
Singles and Doubles
 Championship,
 New York
England

WHERE THE CHIC EAT

Remember, every city has its "power" restaurants and social watering holes. This is a sample of the tastiest morsels around the world.

Breakfast

Polo Lounge, Beverly Hills
Le Restaurant, Regency Hotel, New York
Connaught Hotel, London

Lunch

Bistro Garden, Beverly Hills
Ma Maison, Beverly Hills (Friday only)
Le Cirque, New York
Côte Basque, New York
La Grenouille, New York
21, New York
Four Seasons, New York
Prima Donna, New York
Mortimers, New York (especially Sunday)
Le Reginette, New York (especially Saturday)
Le Relais, New York (especially Saturday)
Marcs Club, London
Harry's Bar, London and Venice
San Lorenzo, London (especially Saturday)
Pontavecchio, London (Sunday only)
Le Relais, Paris
Brasserie Lipp, Paris
Lotti Grill, Paris
Da Bice, Milan

THE BEVERLY HILLS STYLE

Locke Ober, Boston
Le Lion D'or, Washington, D.C.
Tony's, Houston

Tea

Mayfair Regent, New York
Ritz, London
Plaza Athenée, Paris
Cova, Milan
Peninsula, Hong Kong
Trumps, Los Angeles

Cocktails

Polo Lounge, Beverly Hills
Mayfair Regent, New York
Plaza Athenée, Paris
Hassler Villa Medici, Rome

Dinner

Morton's, Beverly Hills
Spago, Beverly Hills
Chasen's, Beverly Hills
Jimmy's, Beverly Hills (especially Saturday)
Matteo's, Beverly Hills (Sunday only)
Joe Stellini, Beverly Hills (early Sunday only)
L'Orangerie, Beverly Hills
Le Cirque, New York
Côte Basque, New York

La Grenouille, New York
Mortimer's, New York
Elaine's, New York
Le Lion d'Or, Washington, D.C.
Robert's, Charleston, S.C.
Prima Donna, New York (late)
Annabell's, London
Marc's Club, London
Harry's Bar, London and Venice
Connaught Grill, London
Claridge's, London
Stresa, Paris
Maxim's, Paris
Latour du Jour, Paris
Kais Bistro, Munich
The Jockey Club, Madrid
The Calala Room, Rome
Da Bice, Milan
The Melting Pot, Johannesburg
Tony's, Houston
The Mansion on Turtle Creek, Dallas
The Odeon, New York
The Ritz Carlton, Boston

Digestivos . . .

DANCIN' TO THE DISCO BEAT!

The "best" disco's for a bit of after-dinner fun and "chic" people watching.

Annabell's, London
Tramps, London
Le Club, New York
Doubles, New York
Visage, New York
Area, New York
Jimmy's, Monte Carlo
Regine's, Marbella
Hippopotamus, Rio de Janiero
Gil's, Rome
Hippopotamus, Paris
Pisces, Washington, D.C.

WHERE THE CHIC DANCE AND CLIMB
(AS IN "SOCIAL") THEIR SOCIAL FEET

Party invitations you want to get and will ALWAYS accept.

P.S. If you don't know where some of these are, it's up to you to find out.

The White House
Any Notable Celebrity
Grace Robbins
Sandra and Ricky Di Portanova
Swifty Lazar's Oscar Party
Costume Institute Dinner
Mary Lou Whitney's Saratoga Dinner Dance
Malcolm Forbes
The Swan Ball
The Lexington Ball
Rex and Comus Ball
The Racing Museum Ball
The Opera Ball
The Harry Platt Annual Party
The Bachelors Cotillion
The International Red Cross Ball
The Red Cross Ball
The Crystal Ball
The Coconuts
Broadlands

CHIC, SINGLE, AND IMPORTANT

The right marriage can propel you straight from a nobody to the "Most Wanted List." You can be sure then when Leona (Helmsly), Yvonna (Trump), and Bobo (Rockefeller) changed their last names (through marriage), they also changed their worlds.

The following are the chicest, richest, and most important singles in The Style-Setting World. This list, presented in no particular order, can, of course, change at the drop of a diamond.

Josephine Abercrombie
Joanne Herring
Lupe Murchison
Joan Weingarten Schnitzer
Kenneth Schnitzer, Sr.
Kenneth Schnitzer, Jr.
William Polk
Olivier Chandon
Sally Phipps
Susie Phipps
Sir Tobias Clarke
Lord George Weidenfeld
Ian Hamilton
Tony Forstmann
Robert de Rothschild
Baroness Philippine de Rothschild
Maria Shriver
Caroline Kennedy
Arlene Walsh
Peter Ausnit
Ted Kennedy
Lindsey Owen-Jones
Ralph Destino
Mark Goodson
Steven Bechtel
Mok Flick
John Clark Gable

The Honorable True Davis Jr.
James Auchincloss
John Kennedy, Jr.
Lee Radziwill
Hugh Auchincloss
Peter Duchin
John Carl Warnecke
James Jennings Sheeran
Natalie Hocq
Sherry Lansing
Lewis Rudin
Alan Loeb
Carolyn Farb
Mark Taper
Lily Auchincloss
Harry Platt
John Warner
Governor Jerry Brown
Carina Courtwright
Jere Engelhard
Michael Butler
Jean Trousdale
Alexander Papamarkou
Arianna Stassinopoulos
Bootsie Barth
Brooke Astor
Principe Francesco Di Sirignano

Mark Hopkinson
Princess Yasmin Khan
Catherine Oxenberg
Maria-Jose Pagliai
John Peden
Peter Jay Sharp
Lally Weymouth
Prince Alfonso Hohenloe
Prince Andrew
Prince Edward
Percival Savage
Davina Phillips
Lady Sarah Armstrong-Jones
Paul Albou
David Cicureil
Judith Belisha

Judy Mazel
Henry McIlhenny
Robert McNamara
Stavros Niarchos
William S. Paley
Count Giovanni Volpi di Misurat
Jill Cashman
Brenda Johnson
Jerry Buss
Patrick Terrail
Carol Connors
Jay Bernstein
Jane Glassman
Contessa Cohen
David Cicurel

THE CHIC-EST OF THE RICHEST

Among the Forbes 400 there are those that do "stand out."

Gordon Peter Getty
Caroline Hunt Schoellkoph
Philip F. Anschutz
Milton Petrie
Perry Richardson Bass and sons
Sid, Edward, Robert and Lee
Preston Robert Tisch
A. Alfred Taubman
Richard Mellon Scaife
Malcolm Stevenson Forbes
Walter Hubert Annenberg

Henry John Heinz
Donald John Trump
William S. Paley
Katharine Graham
Max Martin Fisher
Dominique de Menil
Peter Sharp
Stephen Muss
Robert Adam Mosbacher
Nelson Doubleday, Jr.

TO HAVE AND HAVE NOT EARMARKS OF A STYLE SETTER; OR THINGS YOU WILL FIND AMONG THE POSSESSIONS OF EVERY "STYLE SETTER"

A Galanos and a Valentino couture something
A Savile Row custom suit
A Mariani suit
Custom-made shirts
A Paul Stuart custom-made tie
Gucci loafers
Artioli shoes
An Audemars Piquet, Patek Philippe, or a Vacheron Constantin watch
A Mont Blanc Diplomat pen
Lalo or Pineider stationery
A Nikon F-3 camera with a 35mm single-lens reflex
A Dunhill or Savinelli pipe
A Purdey shotgun
Hermes luggage
Hermes shoes with matching scarf
A Zuber scenic wallcovering
Frette Irish Linen sheets
Ludwigsburg dessert service for six
Spode/Royal Worcester bone china
Buccellati sterling flatware
Steuben and Baccarat crystal
Jewelry from Bulgari, Harry Winston, and David Webb

Late/Great News!

If you would like to become a member of THE BEVERLY HILLS STYLE CLUB, or receive information on my other BEVERLY HILLS STYLE activities and programs:

- THE BEVERLY HILLS STYLEBUILDER Workbook (and Preprinted Fulfillment Aid Cards, 3x5)
- The Home Miracle-Worker (Lotte Berke Home Method Videocassette and Guidebook)
- THE BEVERLY HILLS STYLE Home Makeup Consultation and Starter Cosmetic Kit
- The Synonymee Home Shopper/Fashion Guide
- "Cookin Up a Lot More Fun" Resource Guide (More Party Ideas, Recipes and the Where to Find It) or The Cook-Off
- Your Home Chic Home (THE BEVERLY HILLS STYLE Home Decorating Consultation/Program)
- Le Chic Seen Comprehensive Roster

Please send a self-addressed, stamped envelope to:

THE BEVERLY HILLS STYLE
Information Please
270 North Canon Drive
Beverly Hills, CA 90212

Sources of Quoted Material

Candice Bergen: "The Power of Personality," *The New York Times Magazine*, September 23, 1984.

George Burns: *How to Live to Be 100 or More*, G. P. Putnam's Sons, 1984.

J. M. Clark: *Journal of Political Economics*, October 1927.

Jimmy Connors: *New York Post*, September 1, 1984.

George Cukor: *Beauty and Women*, William Morrow, 1984.

Catherine Deneuve: "The Power of Personality," *The New York Times Magazine*, September 23, 1984.

Benjamin Disraeli: *How to Win Friends and Influence People*, Dale Carnegie and Dorothy Carnegie, Simon and Schuster, 1981.

Stefan Edberg: *New York Post*, September 1, 1984.

Dolly Parton: *Playboy Interview*, Playboy, 1981.

Jane Pauley: *Current Biography*, 1980.

Don Rickles: *Cosmopolitan* "Round-Up," August 1984.

Arnold Schwarzenegger: *Current Biography*, 1979, from an article in *Family Health*, December 1977.

Talia Shire: *New York Post*, September 1, 1984, from *Hollywood Dynasties* by Stephen Farber and Marc Green, Deleliah Books, 1984.

John Travolta: *Photoplay*, January 1980.

Raquel Welch: *Raquel—The Raquel Welch Total Beauty and Fitness Program*, Holt, Rinehart, and Winston, 1984.